T0108435

LOVE IS L

LOVE IS LIKE FIRE

The Confession of an Anabaptist Prisoner

PETER RIEDEMANN

Written at Gmunden, Upper Austria
between 1529 and 1532

EDITED BY
EMMY BARTH MAENDEL

PLOUGH PUBLISHING HOUSE

Published by Plough Publishing House
Walden, New York
Robertsbridge, England
Elsmore, Australia
www.plough.com

Plough produces books, a quarterly magazine, and Plough.com to encourage people and help them put their faith into action. We believe Jesus can transform the world and that his teachings and example apply to all aspects of life. At the same time, we seek common ground with all people regardless of their creed.

Plough is the publishing house of the Bruderhof, an international Christian community. The Bruderhof is a fellowship of families and singles practicing radical discipleship in the spirit of the first church in Jerusalem (Acts 2 and 4). Members devote their entire lives to serving God, one another, and their neighbors, renouncing private property and sharing everything. To learn more about the Bruderhof's faith, history, and daily life, see Bruderhof.com. (Views expressed by Plough authors are their own and do not necessarily reflect the position of the Bruderhof.)

Text translated by Kathleen Hasenberg from Robert Friedmann, ed., *Glaubenszeugnisse oberdeutscher Taufgesinnter* II (Gütersloh: Verlag Gerd Mohn, 1967), 1–47, a diplomatic reproduction of the original German manuscript in the Brünn (Brno) Staatsarchiv, Codex 599, fol. 348–477. Scripture references are from Friedmann's edition. Cover image: *Saint John the Baptist preaching in the Wilderness*, c.1633–50 (oil on canvas), Pieter Brueghel the Younger / Private Collection / Photo © Christie's Images / Bridgeman Images.

A catalog record for this book is available from the British Library
Library of Congress Cataloging-in-Publication Data previous edition:
Riedemann, Peter, 1506–1556.
      [Glaubenszeugnisse oberdeutscher Taufgesinnter.
Selections. English]
Love is like fire: the confession of an Anabaptist prisoner: written at
Gmunden, Upper Austria, between 1529 and 1532 / Peter Riedemann; translated and edited by the Hutterian Brethren [from Robert Friedmann, ed., Glaubenszeugnisse oberdeutscher Taufgesinnter II...1–47].
      p. cm.
Includes bibliographical references.
ISBN 0-87486-058-x
      1. Hutterian Brethren—Doctrines. 2. Anabaptist—Doctrines. 3. Reformation—Austria. I. Friedmann, Robert, 1891–1970. II. Hutterian Brethren (Rifton, N.Y.) III. Title.
BX8129.H8R4813 1993
230'.43—dc20   93–4668
                                                                                CIP

LOVE IS LIKE FIRE –
when it is first kindled in a person,
small troubles and temptations smother
and hinder it; but when it really burns,
having kindled an eagerness for God,
the more temptations and tribulations meet it,
the more it flares, until it overcomes and consumes
all injustice and wickedness.

Peter Riedemann

CONTENTS

INTRODUCTION

Stuart Murray

U NLIKE EARLIER radical movements, whose writings were suppressed and eradicated, the sixteenth-century Anabaptists have bequeathed a rich legacy to future generations. The Hutterites in particular have preserved hundreds of hymns, letters written from prison, encouraging responses by church elders, and confessions of faith.

Peter Riedemann's *Love Is Like Fire* falls into this last category. Some years later he would write a much longer and more detailed confession, which would be adopted by the Hutterian Brethren as their community's statement of faith and practice, but this

Stuart Murray, author of The Naked Anabaptist *and other books, is chair of the Mennonite Trust in the United Kingdom and has a PhD in Anabaptist hermeneutics.*

earlier confession by a courageous young prisoner reveals very clearly his passions and priorities.

Unlike many sixteenth-century texts, this confession is concise and eminently readable. This is deliberate. Riedemann writes, "I do not want to make my message too long-winded and thus too tedious to pay attention to." Much of the confession consists of expositions of creedal statements shared by all Christians, amply illustrated with biblical quotations and the rehearsing of biblical narratives. Riedemann's prose is lucid, passionate, and often poetic.

It is sometimes claimed that the early Anabaptists were non-creedal. They certainly preferred confessions to creeds: creeds were fixed, focused on beliefs rather than practices, and were so often used to anathematize others, whereas confessions were provisional, open to further revelation, and included issues of discipleship as well as doctrine. But many early Anabaptist communities made use of the traditional creeds to instruct their members, and many writers used them as a framework for their tracts and treatises. Riedemann employs this strategy. His confession deviates from this framework on several occasions in order to explore issues about which he was especially passionate or to challenge traditional beliefs and practices, but much of the confession is an exposition of traditional creedal affirmations.

ANOTHER FEATURE of Anabaptist spirituality is the role of narrative. Stories have been passed on down the generations and have profoundly shaped Anabaptist communities, and Anabaptists have paid particular attention to the narrative sections of scripture. So it is not surprising that Riedemann, as he expounds creedal statements, does so in narrative mode. Some sections of his confession consist in a straightforward and winsome rehearsal of the biblical narrative – the creation story, the fall of humanity, and the life of Jesus. The section on Jesus Christ is of particular significance. Traditional creeds say almost nothing about the life of Jesus, passing immediately from "born of the virgin Mary" to "suffered under Pontius Pilate," with only a comma representing what happened in the intervening thirty-three years. One of the most important legacies of the Anabaptist tradition is its insistence that the life of Jesus is not just an incidental precursor to his death and resurrection but of paradigmatic significance for those who would follow him. Riedemann summarizes the narratives in the Gospels and concludes: "He has gone before us so that we may follow in his footsteps."

In our contemporary postmodern and post-Christendom culture, people prefer narrative over doctrinal claims. Many people still respect Jesus and are intrigued by his life and teaching despite their disdain for the church. And people find the language of "following" (typical of Anabaptist writings) helpfully humble and invitational. Although some of Riedemann's language may seem rather dated, these central motifs are not.

Love Is Like Fire contains potent and evocative images. Commenting on the cosmic conflict that underlies the biblical story, Riedemann declares that "Satan had bound us so tightly with his ropes and stood like an armed man" but God "sent the strong hero, Jesus Christ our Lord, against whom no one can prevail," who "burst the chain and the prison that held us." Most Anabaptists have been committed to nonviolence, but their writings do not shy away from the reality of spiritual warfare. Riedemann recognizes that biblical interpretation is also a battleground: "There is a single phrase in scripture that the whole world holds on to and brings up triumphantly here and there, thinking that with this they have won the battle." But he is convinced that careful exegesis will counter false understandings and writes, "If one looks at it thoroughly, it strikes them from their perch."

Throughout his confession there is certainly evidence of Riedemann's thorough exegesis. In some places his attention to detail may result in over-exegesis of particular biblical passages, but this is a young man who has immersed himself in the scriptures. His confession has a discernible bias towards Johannine texts (and, like others in the sixteenth century, he draws occasionally on Apocryphal books – Tobit and Esdras), but he has a broad-based biblical knowledge. He not only reflects deeply on specific texts but weaves together various biblical passages to support and illustrate his teaching. This is a challenge to contemporary churches, many of which are characterized by biblical illiteracy.

ALTHOUGH RIEDEMANN uses the framework of the traditional creeds, his confession emphasizes beliefs and practices that were characteristic of Anabaptism. He affirms the key Reformation insight that "through faith in Christ we become devout and just before God – as a gift," but he insists that "faith is a power that works righteousness and easily carries out all God's will." The grace of God not only wipes away past sins but empowers disciples to live as followers of Jesus. Anabaptists tended to place greater reliance than most of their contemporaries on the work of the Holy Spirit and the capacity that the Spirit gives ordinary people to live as faithful disciples of Jesus. In another poetic passage, Riedemann writes: "He is a father to the poor and miserable, strength to the weak, comfort to the mourning, a guide to the truth for those who go astray, a light to those who sit in darkness. He raises the fallen and gives all the varied gifts of God: quiet rest to those who labor, and coolness and stimulation in the heat of distress and affliction."

The subjects on which Anabaptist prisoners were most frequently questioned were baptism and the Lord's Supper, so it is not surprising that Riedemann devotes considerable attention to these topics. God had given detailed instructions about baptism, as he did to Noah in relation to the ark (Riedemann uses this story, as Peter does, to illustrate the meaning of baptism). He explains why one of the New Testament passages used to justify infant baptism (Acts 16:23–33) is wrongly interpreted for this purpose, and insists that "infant baptism is no baptism at all, but unnecessary washing" with no biblical basis. He concludes: "Let no one rely on being able to say he baptizes infants with good intentions, for God wants his will to stand, not ours." Baptism, Riedemann teaches, is a response to the proclamation of the gospel and a commitment to discipleship.

In a post-Christendom context, some have argued that this issue no longer carries the freight it did in the sixteenth century. Infant baptism today may be as countercultural as believer's baptism was then. And advocates of either form of baptism no longer tend to insult each other in such lurid ways. But perhaps we still need to pay attention to Riedemann's central point: no matter how honorable may be the pastoral concerns of those who baptize infants, and no matter how insightful may be their theological justifications of this practice, if a biblical basis for this cannot be established, "good intentions" are inadequate.

In his teaching on the Lord's Supper, Riedemann explains that this has a horizontal as well as vertical dimension: "It is necessary to consider Christ's death and our death, and also Christ's love and our love." Communion is certainly a remembrance of

Christ's death, but it is also a sign of commitment to Christ and to his people. He concludes this section with a challenging call: "Whoever eats the Lord's bread and drinks from the Lord's cup without first examining himself to see if he is ready to give his life for the truth of the gospel and for his brothers and sisters eats and drinks judgment upon himself."

RIEDEMANN WROTE as a prisoner in a context of persecution. He was experiencing the suffering about which he wrote and knew his readers also faced this. The serious, but not somber, tone of his confession is entirely appropriate in this context. He had interrupted his exposition of the creed with a short parable about the church as a house constructed of many trees that were "cut down, squared, planed, and prepared according to the master's pleasure, and then joined together as a house." He returns to this image at the end of the confession and concludes with an extended parable describing the seven pillars on which the house is built. Throughout this section he urges faithfulness and hope in the face of persecution and suffering.

How do we engage with this in a very different context, in western societies in which suffocation by tolerance is a greater danger than persecution? This context might change, of course, in which case Anabaptist writings will have added poignancy, but in the meantime maybe these writings can help us identify prayerfully with our brothers and sisters in other contexts facing persecution and suffering. The house Riedemann describes is a global community, and we are invited to share in the suffering of other members.

But the dominant theme in this confession is named in its title – love. The first five sections are all about love. Riedemann revels in the love of God for fallen humanity: despite our sin, God "could not restrain and hide his love." And it was love that motivated Jesus: "Out of love to us he did not spare his own life, but gave it for us all." In response, we are to love God wholeheartedly and to love one another – familiar themes but powerfully presented and illustrated with many New Testament texts and references. And, in typically Anabaptist fashion, love for one's enemies (not just one's neighbors) is explicitly included. After all, God's love reaches out to his enemies: "What great love that is! God comforts us, his greatest enemies," writes Riedemann, urging his readers to love their enemies because "love takes hold of people" and this might lead them to the knowledge of God.

In a deeply conflicted world we need to hold on to this hope and embrace this response. And we need to heed Riedemann's warning that "love is like fire":

> When it is first kindled in a person, small troubles and temptations smother and hinder it; but when it really burns, having kindled an eagerness for God, the more temptations and tribulation meet it, the more it flares, until it overcomes and consumes all injustice and wickedness. But when love is not practiced, when one grows lazy and careless, it flickers out again; one's heart grows cold, faith declines, and all good works cease. . . . Love flows from faith; for where there is no faith there cannot be love, and where there is no love there cannot be faith. The two are so entwined that one cannot be pleasing to God without the other.

SETTING THE STAGE

THE ANABAPTIST MOVEMENT sprang from the Reformation. In the midst of the theological debates that began when Martin Luther published his ninety-five theses in 1517, three men in Zurich, Switzerland, took a radical step in 1525: they baptized one another.

The Catholic Church of the sixteenth century was powerful and corrupt. Common people were unable to read the Bible for themselves, and the clergy grew rich on their tithes and taxes. The first Anabaptist leaders were well educated and able to read the Bible in the original Greek and Hebrew. They concluded that much of Catholic doctrine – including infant baptism, transubstantiation, worship of saints, and the sale of indulgences – was false teaching.

The movement spread rapidly through the German-speaking world. Rulers in church and government saw their authority threatened. They arrested

Anabaptists, banished them, and forbade them to preach, but were unable to quell the movement. It wasn't long before "rebaptism" was punishable by death. Yet in spite of persecution the movement continued to spread.

PETER RIEDEMANN was one of the early apologists of Anabaptism. He is best known for his "Confession of Our Religion, Teaching, and Faith,"[1] written in prison in 1540, which remains the most complete doctrinal statement of the Hutterian church. The shorter document contained in this book was written during an earlier incarceration, before Riedemann joined the Hutterites. About this imprisonment the Hutterian *Chronicle* reports simply:

> In this year of 1529 many brothers were arrested in Upper Austria, and some were executed. Among those arrested was Peter Riedemann, born at Hirschberg in Silesia, a cobbler by trade, who was taken prisoner at Gmunden on St. Andrew's Eve (Nov. 29) in 1529. Although he was tortured through many and various means almost to the point of death, he remained faithful. Finally,

after having lain in prison for over three years, he was freed by the providence of God. [2]

On his release in 1532, Riedemann went to Moravia, where there were several Anabaptist communities. He was soon sent as a missionary to Franconia. He was arrested again and spent another four years in prison. When he returned to the communities in Moravia, he found division and tension between three Anabaptist factions. The *Chronicle* reports: "He told them that since God had helped him out of prison, he wanted, as far as the Lord permitted, to visit all who had been at peace when he left and to find out from each side what had happened." At this point he joined the Hutterite group, led by Jacob Hutter's successor, Hans Amon.

Over the next years, Riedemann spent much time as a missionary in what is now Austria and Germany. He repeatedly sorted out differences between groups and individuals, working to unite the people of God. When Hans Amon died in 1542, Riedemann was called back to Moravia to assist his successor, Leonhard Lanzenstiel. He served in this capacity until his death in 1556 at the age of fifty. Unlike many other early Anabaptist leaders, Peter

Riedemann died at home of natural causes, having spent a total of nine years in prison for his faith.

RIEDEMANN was clearly well versed in the Bible. It is unlikely that he had a copy with him in prison – although Bibles were being printed they were still very large and expensive – but the number of passages he quotes suggests that he had memorized many verses.

In this book, Riedemann includes Anabaptist views on two of the most controversial topics of his day: baptism and the Lord's Supper. He is scathing in his criticism of Catholicism, personified in the pope, whom he calls the Antichrist. If this sounds extreme to the modern ear, it should be remembered that the Anabaptists were dying for their beliefs and Riedemann himself had just been tortured "almost to the point of death." They believed they were living in the last times, of which John says: "This is the last hour; and as you have heard that the Antichrist is coming, even now many antichrists have come. This is how we know it is the last hour" (1 John 2:18).

Riedemann was one of the most prolific early Anabaptist writers. Almost forty of his letters have been preserved – letters written to encourage members in prison, and reports and admonitions written in his capacity as a leading minister. These letters reveal many details of his life and the life of the church.[3] The *Chronicle* says of him: "Both in prison and in the church community, he wrote many beautiful Christian songs, spiritual and biblical, for he was rich in all the secrets of God. The gift of God's Word flowed from him like running water and brimmed over. All who heard him were filled with joy."[4]

Emmy Barth Maendel

THE LOVE OF GOD

GOD IN HIS ALMIGHTY POWER and divine nature hovered in the wind before there was a place to stand and before the foundation of the world was laid; he, the infinite being, was alone in his glory. It seemed to him not enough to be alone, however, as there was nothing to praise and glorify his name, for he wanted praise. So in his wisdom, which endures forever and never changes, he created heaven and earth and filled them with his glory – that is, with all creation, the work of his hands in which we recognize his invisible being and eternal power, if we note and observe it. On looking at it, he declared that everything was very good, made according to his will and without blemish. But among them all there was no creature able to give him the praise he wanted, so he said, "Let us make human beings in our image," that

Gen 1:2

Gen 1:1

Rom 1:20

Gen 1:31

Gen 1:26

is, beings who are perfectly pure and completely without blemish.

Gen 1:27–28   Then he made a man and a woman and gave them dominion over all the work of his hands, except the tree of life and of the knowledge of good and evil. *Gen 2:17*   Regarding this tree, he said, "When you eat of it you shall die." But the human beings whom God had made for his praise soon turned away and forgot their Creator's command and all the good things he had given them. They exchanged obedience for *Gen 3:6*   disobedience and ate of the forbidden fruit. This caused them to fall, and their descendants also, for *Gen 3:17–18*   the wrath of God came over them. As a result the earth, too, came under a curse, and as a punishment bore thistles and thorns where they had hoped for good. God had expected goodness and obedience from them, but they had been disobedient and caused thistles and thorns to grow. Therefore eternal death and damnation came over them and all their descendants, and it became impossible for any of them to attain what the one man, Adam, had lost – that is, God's favor and grace; for the wrath of God had come upon them and they lay in the power of death under sin, as under a heavy load that none of them could lift. Only the one eternally powerful

God, against whom they had sinned, could do so through his dearly beloved Son.

But God in his very great wrath over us could not restrain and hide his love. This was impossible, for he himself is love. So he had to show himself and make himself known, and extend love to the human race, and after the curse give comfort once more through his promise. In order that man might have comfort and hope, he said to the serpent, "I will put enmity between your seed and the woman's seed, and her seed will crush your head." This seed is Christ our Savior, who crushed the serpent's head, that is, robbed the devil of his power and dominion. *Gen 3:15*

What great love that is! God comforts us, his *Rom 5:10* greatest enemies, with such a glorious and wonderful promise to free us from death (which we had willfully deserved) and give us everlasting life freely, without our earning or deserving it. So loving is his compassion! Like a spring that overflows, his mercy flows over all who desire it, calling them to this grace and saying, "Everyone who is thirsty, come *Isa 55:1* to the water, and those of you who have no money, come buy wine and milk without price!" Who has ever shown anyone such love as the ruler of all has shown, even to those who despised him? He still

Heb 2:14

---

cares daily for them, and gives them food and drink, clothing, and all they need, also strength of body.

1 Cor 4:7 Truly, what can we have that we did not receive from him? And what could we achieve that was not done by God beforehand and given us? Yet who is thanked less for a gift than the One from whom everything comes, the One who cares for us as a mother does for the child at her breast, and wants nothing evil to befall us, but wants to save us from it all, if only we listen to his voice? For as a bird cares for its young,

Ps 50:15 he watches over us to help us, saying, "Call upon me
Ps 91:15 in the day of trouble; I will hear you and help you." He is a faithful God who soon forgets all our transgressions and favors us with his noblest gifts.

Rom 8:32 God's love is seen in that he did not spare his dearly beloved only Son, but sent him into the world

1 John 4:10 and gave him up to death as atonement for our sin. What great love that is! He makes his only Son whom he loves alive again in us who were dead, and leads us to his kingdom. What more should he have done than he has already done, or what more should

Rom 8:32 he have shown us than he has already shown? God wants to give us everything with him. But not only that; he has already given himself to us to be our

John 1:12 Father and accepted us as his children by freely forgiving our sins. We have not repaid him for this, nor does he want any recompense except that we believe in his name and in Jesus Christ his Son, whom he sent to be the Savior of the world.

1 John 4:14
John 6:29

THE LOVE OF CHRIST

John 1:1–3

CHRIST JESUS, the eternal Word of God Most High, was with the Father before the creation of the world and made all things

Prov 8:23

Prov 8:30

together with his Father. As it is written, "Before the world was, I was, and rejoiced in his presence continually, and when he prepared all things I helped him, for through him all things are made, and nothing was made without him." Everything that has been made, however, has being and remains in him and

John 1:11–12

through him will once more be perfected. He came from above to what was his own, but they did not receive him; but to those who received him he gave the power to become children of God. What great love that is! Christ Jesus, the eternal Father's Son, left the glory beside the Father which he had had

Phil 2:7

before the world was made and came into the world in the form of a servant, endured poverty, temptation, and suffering to set us free from the yoke of misery and servitude. The lord of all lords and king of all kings became poor for our sake that we might become rich in him. We see the love of Christ in that he gave his life for us and suffered death to free us, who were guilty of death. For it is written, "No one has greater love than to give his life for his friend, and you are my friends, if you do all that I command you. I lay down my life in order to receive it again. No one takes it from me, but I lay it down myself." Christ had such love for us that he gave his life and suffered the most humiliating death, namely death on the cross. Thus he became a curse for our sakes, for it is written, "Cursed be everyone who hangs on a tree." *2 Cor 8:9* *1 John 3:16* *John 15:13–14* *John 10:17–18* *Gal 3:13*

How could he have a greater love than this: he suffered so much poverty and misery, and shed his blood in death and so broke down the middle wall of partition and wiped out all that was written against us. He made a sure path to the Father for us and earned for us the Father's favor. See how he spared no effort but did all that was necessary for our blessedness simply so that we might find joy with God and that he might cast off the heavy load that had lain upon us. We could rid ourselves of this in no other way than through him, since Satan had bound us so tightly with his ropes and stood like an armed man, *Eph 2:14* *Col 2:14* *Eph 3:12* *Luke 11:21* keeping us in his power until the appointed time of grace came to us from God, when he sent the strong hero, Jesus Christ our Lord, against whom no one *Heb 2:14–15* can prevail. He took away Satan's power, burst the *Eph 4:8* chain and the prison that held us, and forced Satan *Luke 1:68* to obey him. He redeemed us, his people, in order that we might cleave to him alone and serve him with all our hearts.

Now, all who recognize the love of God the Father and of his dearly beloved Son, and take to heart the great grace that has come to us through him, will truly set their hearts to serve him, obey *Ps 1:2* his commandments, and delight in them by day and *Ps 119:119* night; they will treasure and love the testimony of their God, and have no fear of what may happen to them as a result. They will let nothing hinder them *Rom 8:35–37* in this or turn them aside: as it is written, "What can separate us from the love of God – can tribulation or death, hunger or thirst, heat or frost, fire, water, or sword? As it is written, we are killed all day long and are counted as sheep for slaughter, but in all this we more than overcome for the sake of him who loved us." Such people, however, will watch carefully over their witness to the Lord, and will hold unhindered to God's will against their own will, which they

give to die with Christ. They strangle and kill it, so *Eph 4:23*
that their whole will is changed and renewed, and
they become a new creation in Christ. They put on
Christ and truly surrender themselves to God. Just *Rom 6:19*
as previously they surrendered to sin, obeying it and
serving it, and going from one sin to the next, now,
after having recognized God, they give themselves
and their bodies to God as weapons of righteousness *Rom 6:13*
that they may be holy. Now they no longer live, but *Gal 2:20*
Christ lives in them and brings to perfection everything in them that is pleasing to God, so that they
may praise God with an honest heart. For the true
praise of God is to keep his testimony and love his
name wholeheartedly.

LET US LOVE GOD

1 John 4:19

LET US LOVE GOD; for he loved us first and sent his Son into the world, through whom he has made us holy and sanctified us

1 Pet 2:5
1 John 5:3

to be a holy priesthood, to offer spiritual sacrifices pleasing to him through Jesus Christ. This is the love of God: that we keep his commandments. And his

1 John 2:4

commandments are not burdensome. But whoever says he loves God and does not keep his commandments is a liar. In such a person there is no truth, for

1 John 4:16

whoever loves God remains in God and God in him.

1 John 3:24

We recognize that we remain in God and he in us if we keep his commandments.

Deut 6:4–5

The chief of all God's commandments is, "Hear, O Israel, the Lord your God is one. You must cleave to him, serve him, and love him with all your heart, all your mind, all your soul, and all your strength." So to love God is the fulfillment of all his commands, and to love him with all my powers is to

honor him with all my works and to give him praise.   *1 Cor 10:31*
This means that in all I do and want to do, I look   *Col 3:17*
first to see whether I seek to increase God's praise
in it. If I find that he will be praised by a deed, I joyfully carry it out for God's sake, regardless of the
consequences for me. Where that is not so – where
I do not find God's praise in it – it is useless work. I
should leave it undone in order that God's name not
be profaned in my work (regardless of who becomes
my enemy because of it), and so that what I do may
be done or left undone in God.

To love God with my whole soul means to watch   *Eph 4:29*
all the words I speak so that they serve for God's
praise and the edification and betterment of my
neighbor, as Paul teaches. One should speak words   *1 Cor 14:5, 12*
that are gracious to listen to, necessary, and beneficial
for the body of Christ; words that accord with faith   *1 Pet 4:11*
and serve to confess and testify to the Son of God,
heedless of grumblers – as it is written, "I believe   *2 Cor 4:13*
and so I speak." For all speech that comes from
faith brings betterment and merits God's Spirit and
praise. But if I consider my words and find neither
God's praise nor the betterment of my neighbor, I
should stop, as James teaches, keeping my tongue   *Jas 1:26*
in control, and remain silent, lest my words grieve
God's Holy Spirit; for the wise man says, "Where   *Prov 10:19*

there are many words, lies are not lacking." This is enmity to God and cannot come from truth. Hence the Holy Spirit teaches us, saying, "Do not accustom your mouth to indecent words, for they give rise to sinful thoughts."

Sir 23:7–15

Matt 22:37

To love God with all my heart and soul means that in all my thoughts I praise God, and give no room to sinful thoughts that arise from my flesh, nor listen to them, but fight against them with all my power, and through God's mercy turn to the throne of grace and cry for help and deliverance: "O Lord, free me from this body of death, and do not let the enemy overcome me! Come quickly to help me!" In this way the devil with all his wickedness is overcome. This is the good fight God wants us to fight, the fight in which he has placed us. Only those who fight honestly will receive the crown.

Rom 7:24

Ps 40:13–14

Ps 70: 1–2

2 Tim 4:7–8

Those who love God with their whole heart, mind, soul, and strength would rather be dead to the world, and would rather die than entertain for even a short time a useless or vain thought. They will be silent lest they bring forth words and deeds that profane God's precious name. It befits us to have such love for our God and Christ – not only with our words, but with power, for he dearly loved us first in his Son, and showed us great kindness. For not everyone who says, "I love God" (and everyone says this) really does love God, but only those who show it in power. As is written, "Anyone who loves *John 14:23* me keeps my word and walks in my precepts." Such love works God's work and makes us alive in faith. Whoever loves like this is born of God. *1 John 4:7*

LET US LOVE
ONE ANOTHER

1 John 4:20–21

N OW, IF WE LOVE HIM who gave us birth we should also love one who is born of him, that is, if we love God we should love our brother too. Whoever says he loves God and does not love his brother is a liar, for how can he love God, whom he cannot see, if he does not love his brother, whom he sees. So the godly person *Rom 12:10* should also have brotherly love, as it is written, "Love one another with brotherly affection and each serve the other." Christ gave us this command. When he wanted to leave the world and return to the *John 13:34–35* Father, he said to his disciples, "A new commandment I give to you, that you love one another: even as I have loved you, you also love one another. If you have love for one another, people will know you are *John 15:12* my disciples." But brotherly love implies that we *1 Pet 2:21* lay our lives down for each other, just as Christ did for all of us, giving us an example to follow in his footsteps. So I should not live for myself alone, but live to serve my brothers and sisters – not seek my prosperity and betterment, but theirs, my whole life long. Also, I should take care not to let my brother *Rom 14:15, 21* be grieved or weakened by my work or words. For if my word has grieved a brother, I have lacked love. Whoever does not love his brother is still in death *1 John 3:12–18* and darkness, as John writes, "Anyone who does not love his brother is a murderer, and we know that no murderer has eternal life abiding in him." Whoever loves his brothers and sisters, however, passes from death to life. So let us love everyone – not with words and with our tongues, but in deed and truth. For if someone who has the goods of this world sees his brother in want and does not share with him, how can God's love abide in him? It is rather Cain's love that is in him. He was evil and slew his brother, because his works were evil and his brother's upright.

CHRIST, our Master, gave himself completely to us with all he had and kept nothing back. He himself said, "All that I have received from my Father I *John 17:7* have given to you." He has become our own with all that he has, and we have become his, so that he is in us, and so that we live and move in him. In the same way we should give ourselves to our brothers and sisters and keep nothing from them, but gladly give them love, life, and all that is ours in order to become one indivisible body whose head is Christ. *Eph 4:15–16* Those who remain in such love remain in Christ *John 15:5–6* and Christ in them, and they will bring forth much fruit for eternal life. But whoever does not abide in me, says the Lord, will be cast out to wither and be burned. That is the end and the recompense for the hypocritical and ungenuine love of which the world is full.

1 Pet 1:22 Brotherly love should flow generously from pure *Jer 17:10; 20:12* hearts and not be tainted but remain pure. God the Lord knows what is in a person; he searches the heart and mind. Thus neither outward show nor hypocrisy means anything to him, no matter how fine they seem, for God is not deceived. He wants *Ps 51:17* a sincere, renewed heart. As it is written, "A broken and contrite heart you will not despise." God wants to be praised in spirit, heart, and conscience. As he *Isa 1:13–14* is a spirit, he does not look for outward ceremony which is not founded in the heart. That is an abomination to him, however fine and good it seems. What comes from the heart in faith, however, and is *Phil 4:18* carried out in deed is a pleasing and fragrant offering to his glory.

Love your neighbor as yourself. This is the second commandment and is like the first. On these two depend all the law and the prophets. Indeed, the law – you shall not kill, you shall not steal, you shall not bear false witness, you shall not commit adultery, you shall not commit fornication, you shall not defame, you shall not covet, and all other commandments, however many there may be – are fulfilled in the saying, "Love your neighbor as yourself." But love of one's neighbor, as Christ himself teaches, consists in this: what you would like people to do to you, do to them first – then you will fulfill God's law. Now, no one desires evil to befall him; he desires good from all. Therefore, in obedience, we should first show others love, loyalty, and goodness; then they will not speak against the praise of God. In this way we gladly make ourselves of service to all people for Christ's sake, that his name may be praised through us, also by unbelievers, for when they see how we serve they will have no ground for blasphemy. Such love flows from brotherly love, as Peter shows us when he says, "Supplement your faith with virtue, and virtue with modesty, modesty with godliness, godliness with brotherly love, and brotherly love with the love of all. If these things are in you, you will not be lazy or unfruitful in the knowledge

Matt 22:39–40

Rom 13:9

Matt 7:12

2 Thess 1:12
1 Pet 2:12

2 Pet 1:5–8

of God and of Christ." It follows that people who are born of God are inclined to show their neighbors love, loyalty, and all that is good spontaneously and without end.

If you ask, "Who is my neighbor?" listen to Christ's teaching in the Gospel:

Luke 10:30–37   A man went from Jerusalem to Jericho and fell among thieves who beat him and left him wounded and half-dead. Then a priest went the same way, and on seeing him passed by; then a Levite did the same thing. But a Samaritan also went that way, and when he saw him he was moved to compassion. He went to him and poured wine and oil in his wounds, took him to an inn and cared for him. The next morning, before continuing his journey, he took a coin from his purse, gave it to the innkeeper and said, "Look after him, and on my return I will repay you for whatever more you have spent." Which of these is neighbor to the wounded man? The man who showed him compassion.

From this we recognize that we are all one another's neighbor – the one who needs help and the one who offers help. No one is excluded.

But if you want to strive for perfection you must, in order to reach this goal, love those who hate and despise you as well. For Christ taught, "To the men *Matt 5:43–45* of old it was said, 'You shall love your friend and hate your enemies,' but I say to you, love your enemies, do good to those who hate you, bless those who curse you, and pray for those who persecute you, that you may be children of your Father in heaven, who makes his sun rise over the evil and the good and sends rain on the just and the unjust." For that is God's way: through patience he calls sinners to repentance. So *Rom 2:4* the children who have received his Spirit should walk in his footprints and be disciples of God. Paul teaches, "Be followers of God as beloved children." *Eph 5:1* Through patience and through returning good for *Rom 12:17* evil, they should point their enemy to uprightness, *1 Thess 5:15* for it is written, "If your enemy is hungry, feed him; *Rom 12:20* if he is thirsty, give him drink; for in so doing you will heap fiery coals on his head." Perhaps this kindness may affect him so that he considers deeply and turns over a new leaf. He will think, "I treat this man badly, and he repays me with kindness and does all he can to serve me and is my friend. Oh, what am I doing? I want to change and do as he does – leave the evil and pursue the good – for what does it help me to live in wickedness and oppose the will of God?"

When this takes place – when you move a human being to a good conscience – you have helped a soul from death to life, which is sure to be rewarded by God. . . . The evildoer will say in his heart (even though he does not let it be seen), "This man accepts everything patiently that I maliciously do to him, and is so ready to do good to me – he is truly better than I am." In this way your good deeds become a witness to him. But if he does not better himself and repent after such a witness, he increases God's wrath upon him in the day of judgment.

Such love is a band of perfection. When love takes hold of people they are pleasing to God and approved by others. They abide in God, and God in them, and their life and all their work is accomplished in God; for God's clarity enlightens and surrounds them so that they walk in the light of God's grace and are no longer surrounded by darkness. Bright radiance and great light has enlightened their hearts, and they are defended by the Holy Spirit and led with sure conscience to the peace of the saints. Whoever does not have this is blind; groping for the wall, he does not know where he will fall or that the pit of hell is close to him.

Jas 5:20

Rom 2:5

Col 3:14

Isa 59:10

WHAT LOVE IS

A S SO MUCH has already been said about love, we must show what it is like in order that it is better understood, that one may not think he has love when it is only an illusion. Love cannot hide itself, because its nature is light. It must shine and show itself in active work, serving all people and doing good. For love does everyone good. It is ready to serve; it is kind, gentle, patient, humble, pure, temperate, modest, sympathetic, good, compassionate, gracious, lowly, forbearing, loyal, and peaceable. Love is not repulsive; it is not proud, puffed up, boastful, envious, or drunken; it is not self-willed, disobedient, deceitful, quarrelsome, or thieving. Love does not gossip; it is not jealous, irate, or spiteful; it despises no one, but bears all things and suffers all things; it is not vengeful; it does not repay evil with evil; it does not rejoice in

1 Cor 13:4–6

what is wrong, but rejoices in truth. Only love does God's work.

Love is like fire, which goes out before it really ignites if one puts too much wood on it, as those who work with it know. But once it really flares, the more wood one puts on it, the better it burns, so that even houses and whole forests are consumed. When there is no more wood, however, it dies and grows cold. It is the same with love. When it is first kindled in a person, small troubles and temptations smother and hinder it; but when it really burns, having kindled an eagerness for God, the more temptations and tribulation meet it, the more it flares, until it overcomes and consumes all injustice and wickedness. But when love is not practiced, when one grows lazy and careless, it flickers out again; one's heart grows cold, faith declines, and all good works cease. Then *Matt 7:19* one stands like a withered tree fit for the fire, as Jesus himself says. Love flows from faith; for where there is no faith there cannot be love, and where there is no love there cannot be faith. The two are so entwined that one cannot be pleasing to God without the other.

WHAT FAITH IS

FAITH is a certain assurance of what we hope for, a clear revelation and a conviction of things that are not seen, a conquest of the world, the devil, and the flesh. It is a sure guide to God, an assurance of the hope and purification of the heart; through it one becomes completely pure, holy, and godly. But faith is also a justification, because through faith in Christ we become devout and just before God – as a gift. Faith is a power that can do everything – nothing is impossible for it. As Christ testifies, "If you have faith like a mustard seed, say to this mountain, 'Get up from here and cast yourself into the sea,' and it will obey." Or, "Be it done for you as you have believed." Faith is also an assurance of the conscience that it stands firm and trusts God's promise. Thus it is a confirmation of the supplication, for God does not disdain the prayer of the believer, but must grant the request since it comes

Heb 11:1

Rom 3:24

Matt 17:20

Matt 8:13; 15:28

1 John 5:14   from faith. John says, "We are certain that we have received what we have asked him for."

As Paul teaches, faith is a power that works righteousness and easily carries out all God's will. People who say they cannot carry out God's will show that they are not believers but unbelievers, for all *Mark 9:23*   things are possible to those who believe. It is easy for them to walk in the footsteps of Christ, who has said, *Matt 11:30*   "My yoke is easy and my burden light." Those who do not believe consider Christ a liar and accuse him of not meaning it; that is, they accuse him of loading unbearable burdens upon us, although in fact he has placed the very lightest that he could upon us; for he took upon himself and carried a heavy burden which we could neither move nor carry, and he has reduced the burden of all the commandments to one commandment, namely love, that we may the more easily grasp it and reach our goal.

Whoever believes also confirms and testifies that *Hab 2:4*   God is faithful in all his promises. "For he who is righteous through faith shall live." However, it is impossible to believe before one knows God and the strength of his power as well as his love and faith- *Rom 10:14*   fulness to us. Paul writes, "How can they believe before they hear?" Therefore God sent his own Son into the world, who has proclaimed to us the name

of God our Father in order that we can believe and
have hope in God, as it is written: "I will proclaim   *Ps 35:18*
your name to my brothers and sing your praise in
the great congregation." Further, "I have made your   *John 17:26*
name known to them." John writes, "No one has   *John 1:18*
ever seen God; the only begotten Son of the Father
has made him known to us," and, "We have believed   *1 John 1:5*
and bear witness that God is light," and, "We know   *John 21:24*
that our witness is true."

Jesus Christ revealed God's will so clearly that
nothing is left that he has not told us. He went
before us, not with words only but also with deeds
and power, and he has shown us the way to follow
him. For he walked in obedience to his Father unto   *Phil 2:8–11*
death – even death on the cross, which he endured
for our sin. So the Father awakened him again
and raised him up as king over all the kings of the
earth and gave him a name that is over all names;
at the name of Jesus every knee will bow in heaven,
on earth, and under the earth, and all tongues will
confess that God has made him lord of all lords and
king of all kings. His kingdom endures forever and   *Luke 1:33*
has no end, as is written: "I have set my king on   *Ps 2:6*
Zion, my holy hill." Mount Zion is the community
of believers gathered and united in love by the Holy
Spirit through unity of faith, building up those who

are consecrated through the blood of Christ to be a holy house. That is why Christ, after he had risen and before he took possession of heaven, appeared to his disciples and commanded them to be witnesses *Mark 16:15–16* of all they had seen and heard, and said, "Go into all the world and preach the gospel to all creation; whoever believes and is baptized will be saved; but whoever does not believe will be condemned."

Here Christ follows the example of his Father, who created everything in the right order and not in confusion. First he created the earth, and then the grass that came from the earth as food for the cattle, so that they, when made, might have fodder and not suffer want. The cattle, however, were food for man, prepared before man was made, so that each created being would have what it needed before it actually was. God acts wisely in all his works and *Gen 1:31* sees that everything is rightly ordered. Christ did the same: when he wanted word of his good deeds to be spread among the children of men, he first sent the disciples, saying, "Go!" and commanded them to preach the gospel. They did not go of themselves, but through being sent they received strength for their task and were not unfruitful. In the same way *Rom 10:14–18* Paul writes: "How can they hear without preachers; how can they preach before they are sent? Yet, have they not heard? Their voice has gone out into all the world, its sound to the end of the earth." Thus faith comes from hearing, hearing through preaching, but preaching through the Word of God.

PROCLAMATION
OF THE WORD

THE VOICE of those whom God draws, teaches, and sends is heard by the heart of the believer. They do not speak their own words but God's, so people gladly listen to them and follow his word not only with their ears, but with their hearts. Jesus says, "My sheep hear my voice; they do not listen to the voice of a stranger. I go before them, and they follow me, for I know who are mine, and they know me." From this we can recognize that up till now many – if not all – have run without being sent by God, and have not been shepherds of the sheep, but hirelings who sought their own gain more than that of the sheep. As no betterment results from their preaching, they have not proclaimed God's Word but their own fabrication (even though their deceit was covered up with godly words). That is why the sheep did not

John 10:3–5

John 10:14

hear them. For when God's Word is proclaimed in *Isa 55:11*
its purity, it will not return empty but will accom-
plish all that is commanded of it, says the Lord.
Because Christ wanted to send to his sheep shepherds who would faithfully pasture them, he said to
his disciples, "Go out into all the world, preach, and *Mark 16:15*
proclaim the gospel" – that is, the good news about
him and the good things he has done for us, making
us blessed through his death. Much has already been
said about this elsewhere.

WHAT WE BELIEVE
ABOUT BAPTISM

Matt 10:13–14

"WHOEVER BELIEVES, that is, receives your words, will have your peace come over him, for you proclaim it and I bring it about in him, and he is baptized – that is, he submits to your word and becomes a partaker of my death through killing and mortifying the flesh."

Rom 6:3 This takes place in baptism, as Paul says: "All of us who have been baptized were baptized into Christ's Gal 3:27 death." And again, "All of us who have been baptized have put on Christ." Yes, they have changed and become new creatures in Christ, so that they live from now on no more for themselves but for God through Jesus Christ.

Matt 10:13–15 Whoever does this will be blessed, but whoever does not believe, that is, does not accept your words and the witness to me that you proclaim, makes himself unworthy of it. Then your peace will not remain in him but return to you again. Leave that place and shake the dust from your feet as a witness against it. Truly I say to you, it shall be more tolerable on the day of judgment for Sodom and Gomorrah than for such a person, for he is condemned.

This is Christ's purpose in his advice, as is sufficiently proved in scripture, where each devout heart can rightly recognize what it must do in accordance with Christ's command. But that this knowledge may be better assured, I will quote one more passage (and, for the sake of brevity, omit many others): Peter says, *1 Pet 3:20–21* "It is as it was in the days of Noah during the building of the ark, in which a few, namely eight people, were kept safe in the water through God's word. The counterpart of this ark today is baptism, which saves you, not as the removal of dirt from the body, but as the bond of a good conscience with God." That is, I recognize I have a gracious God who has forgiven my sins, accepted me into the community of his saints as his child, and given me himself as Father; so I may bind myself to him, to walk henceforth in accordance with his will, never again to transgress it as formerly, and ask that my heart become firm in the hope of his grace, and trust God's promise assuredly. That is the bond of baptism, which no infant can make, as it knows neither good nor evil. Thus infant baptism is no baptism at all, but unnecessary washing. For baptism is not what takes place outwardly; it takes place in the renewal of a person's heart and conscience – though afterwards we *Phil 4:3* also receive the outward sign through which we are written in the book of life and are incorporated into the body of Christ and his holy church, the fellowship of saints.

Since Peter says the ark is symbolic of baptism, we ought to examine the symbol to see what it teaches us. God commanded Noah to build the ark for the *Gen 6:13–16* flood. He said, "Make yourself an ark in which you and your household can be saved, because I am going to destroy the world." God told him how to make it: its form, height, length, and breadth, and he gave him the time to do so, namely one hundred and *Heb 11:7* thirty years. Noah obeyed God and did not alter his command, holding in firm faith to what God had *Gen 8:1* told him; he was thus preserved in the ark together with his whole household, as God had promised him. But if he had not listened to God's voice, if he had made the ark a different way, according to his own design and not God's, it would have been of no use to him, and he would have perished with the rest. In the same way, Christ has also commanded and given us true baptism and shown us how it should be done. Whoever listens to his voice and receives baptism in accordance with his command and with firm faith in his promise will be preserved and saved, but whoever does not listen to Christ's voice, neglects baptism, or receives it in a different way from what Christ has commanded, will perish with the unbelieving. For God's will is that we obey his command exactly without altering it. He said to Moses, "See that you follow the plan I showed you on the mountain," but those who from the beginning of the world were disobedient and altered God's command – even if they did so with good intentions – brought punishment upon themselves, as we see in Saul and in the prophet whom God sent to Bethel from Judah. So let no one rely on being able to say he baptizes infants with good intentions, for God wants his will to stand, not ours.

1 Pet 1:5

Exod 25:40
Exod 26:30

1 Sam 15
1 Kgs 12:26–13:5

THE ERROR
OF INFANT BAPTISM

Matt 15:13

CHRIST SAYS, "Every plant which my heavenly Father has not planted will be rooted out." It is clear enough that infant baptism is not from God, but appointed by the Antichrist and son of perdition, the pope. This is clearly seen in the statements of the pope, though the whole world defends it today, thinking they have their safeguard in God's Word. If one really looks at the Word, one sees that infant baptism is as far from the Word as heaven and earth are from each other.

There is a single phrase in scripture that the whole world holds on to and brings up triumphantly here and there, thinking that with this they have won the battle. But if one looks into it thoroughly, it strikes them from their perch. It is this: that the apostle baptized a whole household, in which there

were presumably also children, and that therefore children were baptized. But we are told clearly
which household members were baptized and which
were not. When Paul was imprisoned in Philippi, *Acts 16:25–34*
he was praying in the night, and suddenly an earth-
quake occurred, opening the doors of the prison and
loosening all the prisoners' fetters. When the jailer
awoke from sleep and saw the prison doors open, he
thought the prisoners had escaped, and taking his
sword, he thought to kill himself. But Paul called
out, "Do yourself no harm – we are all here." The
jailer called for a light and rushed in trembling
and said, "Men, what must I do?" Paul said to him,
"Believe in the Lord Jesus!" Then he took them into
his house, washed their wounds, and set food before
them. Then Paul spoke the word of God to him and
his whole household, and he and his whole household believed.

Here we see which household members were baptized: namely, those who had observed the works
of God and believed the words of Paul. It does not
follow that infants were among them. Thus their
whole foundation is built on sand and must fall,
however firmly they believe it stands, and however
cleverly the worldly-wise argue about it. It was not

for nothing that the Lord said of them through the prophets, "The Lord knows the thoughts of man, and they are vain." And again, "He traps the cunning in their own craftiness." The reason for their struggle is that they do not want to come to nothing and humble themselves before God, to seek their own praise no longer, but God's praise. They think by their knowledge they can fathom God's wisdom. So the Lord has allowed them, in the blindness of their hearts, to want to make truth lies and lies truth, to make the straight crooked and the crooked straight, to make light darkness and darkness light.

Ps 94:11

Job 5:13

Isa 5:20

Every sincere and simple heart that loves God can learn from what I have said to distinguish error from truth. I have written briefly, using only a few scripture passages, but there are many more that testify in complete accord, which can be looked up and compared. I have omitted them because I do not want to make my message too long-winded and thus too tedious to pay attention to. May God give grace to all simple hearts and lead them in certainty of his Word, so that they grasp the promised blessedness with all saints through Jesus Christ, his dearly beloved Son. Amen.

2 Thess 2:16

May the eternal God, our compassionate Father, who is a Father of all grace and a God of all comfort, open the eyes and the ears of your minds, that you may see and know his eternal will, which is written in your hearts. Amen.

I BELIEVE IN GOD

I believe in God, the Father almighty,
creator of heaven and earth.

SINCE GOD in his honor and glory was not satisfied to be alone, and since he did not want to be praised except by the work of his hands – to be recognized as father, creator, and source of life – he created man, who was to acknowledge him and rightly praise and thank him through whom he had being, life, protection, food, and support. Since, however, God wanted man to know him, it was necessary for something to be there already in which his power and glory could be seen and known; therefore in the beginning he created heaven and earth. When he said, "Let there be heaven and earth," it was so. But it was dark upon the deeps, so he said, "Let light come out of the darkness," and it took place; there was evening and

Gen 1

---

morning – the first day. After this he separated the waters between the firmament and the earth, and divided the land from the water. He called what was dry "earth" and called the water "sea," and there was evening and morning – the second day. Then God created all manner of green foliage and grass, and there was evening and morning – the third day. Then he created two great lights: the one to light the day, which he called sun, and the other to shine by night, which he called moon, and he gave it stars as helpers. Then evening and morning became the fourth day. Then he created all manner of creeping and four-footed animals, and evening and morning became the fifth day.

God saw that everything he had created on these days was good, and he said, "All I have made is very good," but among all his creatures none was found able to know God in truth and praise him. So God said, "Let us make human beings in our own image." He took a clod of earth and formed a man *Gen 2:7* and placed all created things before him so that he *Gen 2:19–24* could name them, each according to its kind. But no creature was found resembling Adam who could be his helper, so God made Adam sleep and while he slept God took one of his ribs and made a woman of it. When he awoke God placed her before him, and when Adam saw her, he said, "This is bone of my bone and flesh of my flesh; she shall therefore be called woman." For that reason a man will leave father and mother and cleave to his wife, and the two will be one flesh. And evening and morning were the sixth day.

THE FALL OF MAN

ON THE SEVENTH DAY God rested from all his work. Then God made Adam and Eve rulers over all he had created. He placed them in the midst of the garden and said, "All things are subject to you, and you may eat of all the fruits of the garden, except from the tree of the knowledge of good and evil, for as soon as you eat it you will die." When God made them to rule over all creatures, he explained to them that as they were lords over the creatures, God was Lord over them. That was why he had laid down a law for them. Soon after, however, resentment arose in the creatures, so that the serpent, the deceitful devil, said to Eve, "Did God really say 'As soon as you eat the fruit you will die?' It is not so; as soon as you eat you will be as wise as gods and like them." When Eve heard this, she looked at the fruits and desired them, for they

Gen 2:2

Gen 1:28
Gen 2:16–17

Gen 3

looked delicious. Besides, she wanted to be some-body, so she listened to the serpent and ate the fruit and then gave some to Adam as well. But as soon as they had eaten, their eyes were opened and they saw that they were naked – that is, they recognized that they had left God's will, and were stripped of his grace, which had covered them. Beginning to feel ashamed, they reached above them, tore leaves from the fig trees, and made aprons of them to cover their shame. Then they hid themselves under the bushes. In the evening, when it was cool, God's voice called to them, "Where are you, Adam?" But he was silent until God had called three times. Then he answered, "Lord, I have hidden myself, because I am ashamed of my nakedness." God said, "Who told you that? You have clearly eaten from the tree of which I forbade you to eat." Adam answered, "Lord, the woman whom you gave me offered me the fruit, and I ate." Then God said to Eve, "Why have you done this?" She answered, "Lord, the serpent seduced me."

Then God said to the serpent, "Because you have done this, you shall be cursed above all creatures. You shall crawl on your belly your life long, and eat earth, and I will put enmity between your seed and the seed of the woman, and her offspring will bruise your head, but you will bite his heel." And to Eve he said, "As you have listened to the serpent, you shall bear your children in great pain." To Adam God said, "Because you paid more attention to your wife than to me, the earth shall be cursed on your account. It shall bear thistles and thorns for you, and only by the sweat of your brow will you eat bread." And God said: "Man now knows good and evil; he might turn and eat of the tree of life and become like me." So he thrust them out of the garden and set an angel with a fiery sword to guard the gate.

When Adam, in his disobedience, decided to obey God no longer, he found that creation also became disobedient to him. Just as he had disobeyed God's command, the creatures now disobeyed him, and they could only be made to obey once more by using great force. We, too, can only live in obedience to God by denying our carnal will and dying to self, which is achieved with great tribulation and suffering.[5]

A PARABLE

T HERE ARE MANY TREES in a wood. All alike are God's creation and good for building a house, but nothing will come of it unless they first endure the master builder's work: they must be cut down, squared, planed, and prepared according to the master's pleasure, and then joined together as a house. In the same way, there are many people, all alike good creations of God, made for his praise, and all made to serve as God's house in which he wants to live. But the house of God will not be made of everyone, but only of those who accept God's working and discipline: they must be hewn down from all vanity and wickedness, cut with Christ's circumcision, purified in their hearts, and truly surrendered to God the Father to follow Christ. These will be united in the bond of love as a house of God in which he lives. As is written, "You are the temple of the living God." And again, "I will

Hag 1:8

1 Cor 3:16
Rev 21:3

———

44

live and walk in them, and I will be their God, and they shall be my people." We are taught by this and other parables that when we have transgressed, we should submit once more in obedience to God and suffer and bear the discipline by which he makes us fit and pleasing for him to live in.

The purpose of all that has been said so far is to make God's power and might more easily recognizable. Paul also taught that God's invisible nature and eternal power can be recognized in his works since the creation of the world.[6]

Rom 1:20

In all this we see the power of God: how he redeems all his own at the right time; how wonderfully he leads his saints and teaches them what faith has worked in them and what God's power is; and how we should truly rely upon and trust the Lord. So search scripture, and recognize clearly how you can please God. May the eternal God help you to do this with his inexpressible grace and power.

I BELIEVE
IN JESUS CHRIST

I believe in Jesus Christ,
God's own son, our Lord,
who was conceived by the Holy Spirit,
born of the virgin Mary,
suffered under Pilate,
was crucified, died, and was buried.
He descended into hell,
rose from the dead on the third day,
appeared to his disciples, and ascended into heaven.
He sits at the right hand of God, the Father,
from whence we await him,
the coming judge of the living and the dead.

Gen 3:15 WHEN THE IMMORTAL GOD, our faithful Father, wanted to fulfill his promise and send the promised Seed who was to crush the serpent's head – that is, take away the devil's power, destroy his kingdom, and efface his dominion – he sent his eternal Word, who became man in Mary. The angel Gabriel brought the message from God and greeted her, saying, "Hail Mary, O favored one, the Lord is with you!" But she was greatly troubled and pondered the meaning of this greeting. As she stood afraid, the angel comforted her and said, "Do not be afraid, Mary. You will conceive in your womb and bear a son who will be great and will be called the Son of the Most High." Then Mary asked, "How can that be? I have no husband." The angel answered, "The power of the Most High will come from above into you, so he who will be born of you is holy." *Luke 1:26–38*

When Mary heard that it would take place through God, she said, "So be it! See, I am a handmaiden of the Lord." When she submitted herself to the word of the Lord, she conceived through the working of the Holy Spirit and bore for us the Son whom God had promised beforehand through the prophet Isaiah, who had said, "Behold, a virgin will conceive and bear a son whose name will be Immanuel." He came as a light into the world to shine upon those who sit in darkness. As it is written, "The people who sat in darkness have seen *Isa 7:14*

John 1:4–5
John 12:46
Isa 9:2

a great light, and the people who sat in the shadow and power of death have received a great salvation."

Now since the Sun of discernment and under-standing has arisen and the glory of goodness has appeared to us, we should walk in it as children of the light, so that darkness does not lay hold of us again. For whoever walks in darkness does not know where he will fall. But Christ came that we might have the light of life in us and that we might be redeemed from death by his voice. That is why God promised him to us through Moses, his faith-ful servant, and commanded us to listen, saying, "The Lord your God will raise up for you a prophet such as I from among your brothers; him you shall heed." And the soul of anyone who will not give heed to that prophet will be cut off. For God himself commands him to hear, saying, "This is my beloved Son in whom I am reconciled. Listen to him." Yet although he came to his own, those who were his own neither listened to him nor received him. To those who did receive him, however, he gave power to become children of God, born not of the flesh, but of God, through the living Word whom he sent into human hearts. Thus in future no one need say to his brother, "Know the Lord," for all of them who

Eph 5:8–9

John 12:35–36

Deut 18:15–19

Matt 17:5

John 1:11–13

Jer 31:34

have been born like this, high and low alike, shall know him.

Christ was sent that he might be the Savior of all people. He did the will of the Father, quieted the Father's wrath, broke down the dividing wall, and abolished the law. Out of two [Jews and Gentiles] he has made a new man and prepared a sure way to the Father. Through him we have access to the Father in one Spirit and are fellow citizens of the saints and members of God's household, made fit to receive all the glory. He has bought us this inheritance with his blood, which he shed to make us saints and cleanse us from our sins. Through his stripes we have been healed, for he took away all our diseases and bound up the deep wounds made by Satan's hard blows. He has gone before us so that we may follow in his footsteps. He did not revile when he was reviled, nor threaten when he suffered, but he trusted everything to the Father, whose will he carried out, obedient unto death – even death on the cross. Here the just suffered for the unjust, the innocent for the guilty, to lead us to God. Then, when God set such joy before him, he suffered the cross, despising its shame. Look at what great cost Christ won us! He spared neither work nor effort, but willingly laid aside all his glory

1 John 4:14

Eph 2:14–19

Isa 53:5

Phil 2:8

1 Pet 3:18

Heb 12:2

2 Cor 8:9 (for he was Lord of heaven and of earth) and became poor for our sakes to make us rich and whole in

Phil 2:7 him. He took upon himself the form of a servant and made himself servant to everyone. He himself

Matt 20:26–28 said, "I have not come to be served, but to serve." As a mighty king who willingly left his kingdom and took upon himself a low condition, he has shown us by example that whoever is high should become a servant to the one who is low. He commanded, "Whoever wants to be the greatest among you must be the slave of all the others."

Heb 5:8 Christ learned obedience through suffering. Because out of love to us he did not spare his own

Phil 2:9–11 life, but gave it for us all, the Lord raised him again, crowned him with praise and honor, and gave him a name above all names, that at the name of Jesus every knee should bow in heaven, on earth, and in the deep, and every tongue confess that he is Lord.

Heb 1:9 God anointed him with the oil of joy over all his

Acts 2:24, 27 comrades. With a mighty arm he awoke him from death, after it proved impossible for death to keep him. As David said, "You will not permit your holy one to see corruption or leave his soul in hell."

1 Cor 15:6 Therefore he arose with power and appeared to his disciples and was seen by many brothers. But when

the time was fulfilled, he was taken to heaven in the sight of the apostles. There he was set at the right hand of the throne of the Majesty on high (Stephen also saw him seated there), where he waits until all his foes are placed under his feet. We believe he is also there to represent us.

Heb 12:2

Acts 7:55

1 Cor 15:25

WHAT EATING
CHRIST'S FLESH MEANS

John 20:17

WE DO NOT BELIEVE Christ is in bread, nor that he lets himself be handled by every sinner. For when Mary Magdalene wanted to touch him (after the resurrection) he did not let her do so – even though he had cleansed her from all evil and sin. Since he did not permit one whom he had made upright and holy to touch him, how can he want every whore, every avaricious, abusive, impure person to handle him now? For scripture says, "He will not be served by human hands." Now you say, "Christ permitted Thomas to touch him when he said, 'Put your finger here and see my hands, and put out your hand, and place it in the wound in my side; and do not be faithless, but believe.'" It does not follow from this, however, that Thomas touched him, for as soon as he

Acts 17:25

John 20:27–29

heard and saw Christ, disbelief left his heart and he knew Christ was truly arisen. He witnessed to this by saying, "My Lord and my God!" He no longer wanted to touch him, and the text clearly shows that he did not, for Christ says, "Because you saw me, Thomas, you have believed. Blessed are those who have not seen and yet have believed." Thus we see he speaks only of seeing and not of touching.

It does not even matter if one quotes, "Whoever eats my flesh and drinks my blood will live forever." Just look at what comes before and after these words, and you will find what eating Christ's flesh means. Before this it says, "When he had fed the people in the desert and crossed the water, early next morning the people also crossed over, and when they found him they said to him, 'Master, when did you come here?' Christ answered, 'You do not seek me because you saw the signs, but because you ate your fill of the bread; seek for the bread that does not perish but endures eternally in heaven.'" He continued, "Your fathers ate heavenly bread in the wilderness, and they died." We read, "He gave them bread from heaven, and each one ate the bread of the angels." Christ said, "Moses did not give you bread from heaven, but my Father gives you the true bread from

John 6:54

John 6:24–58

Ps 78:24–25

heaven, so that whoever eats it will not die but have eternal life; the bread I give is my flesh, which I shall give for the life of the world."

Now listen carefully: Did flesh and blood come from heaven? You will clearly see that his flesh and blood did not come down from heaven, but he only became flesh in Mary. So Christ is not speaking here of his physical flesh and blood, but of the faith of the living Word of God, who came down from heaven and gives life to the world. Whoever believes this Word and surrenders himself to God as Mary did has already eaten the flesh of Christ. As it is written, *John 14:23* "If anyone believes in me, my Father and I will come and make our home with him." So believing the truth is what it means to eat Christ. Elsewhere we see clearly that he is not speaking of eating his physical flesh and blood, nor does he want us to eat him. The disciples also did not understand. They *John 6:60–63* were appalled at his words, and said, "This is a hard saying; who can listen to it?" meaning "Who wants to eat his flesh?" He answered them, "Do you take offense at this? What then if you will see the Son of man ascend to heaven where he was before? It is the spirit that gives life; the flesh is of no use" – that is, it is no use to eat. But flogged for us, killed, and raised from the dead, it is of very great use to us, and without it we could not be saved. That is why he says, "The words I speak are spirit and life." If they are spirit and life, they are not flesh and blood.

THE ERROR OF THE MASS

Matt 26:26

EVEN THOUGH Christ says, "Take and eat, this is my body," he does not mean we should make a god of it right away, as the belly-preachers do, who misuse these words to please themselves and avoid suffering. They are truly devoted to a god: their stomach. If it were true, as they say, that Christ was eaten in the bread, why then do they need to be worried about damna-*John 6:54* tion? For it is written, "He who eats of me will have eternal life," and God does not regret his gift. Since *John 12:26* Christ says, "Father, I will that where I am, there my servants will also be," so each one who truly receives and eats Christ is certain of his glory. Because they are not certain about God's promise, however, but waver about it, they witness by their deeds that they have neither received nor eaten Christ – that Christ is not there at all.

So the saying "This is my body" must not be understood in such a physical sense. You will hear later how to understand it when I speak of the Lord's Supper. But in order to keep back nothing from you, and to tell you what I really think of your communion bread, I say it is bread upon which the Lord's curse comes, and all who eat it make themselves unclean and cannot come into the Lord's house. Your blessing banishes it from God's sight, as it is written: "Since they transgress my covenant and do not walk in my law, I will curse all their blessings." In short, all the praise rightfully due to the living Christ is taken from him and given to the dead element, bread, which can neither see, hear, nor speak, and is of no use to itself, let alone to any other.

Mal 2:2

But we have a living Christ through whom everything has been made, has being, and is sustained, and from whom each one receives help. He has been appointed by God a judge of the living and the dead. He testifies himself that he does not want his body (with which he ascended into heaven) to remain in bread or in any other place on earth, for he says, "You will always have the poor with you, but you will not always have me." And again, "I am leaving the world and going to the Father." However, he is always near

Acts 10:42

Matt 26:11

John 16:28

us with his almighty divine strength, for he says, "I
Matt 28:20 am with you always, to the end of the world."

WHAT WE BELIEVE ABOUT
THE LORD'S SUPPER

I CANNOT PRAISE and glorify the Lord's Supper enough as it is described figuratively in the Old Testament and kept in the New. When God had afflicted Pharaoh, and then, wanting to plague him still more, decided to strike down the firstborn in the whole of Egypt, he commanded Moses that the people should kill a lamb, take its blood, and smear it on the lintel of their doors, so that when the angel of death came he would not enter and do harm. The lamb was to be a yearling without spot or blemish, and the people were to cook it without water – roast it. Where there were not enough people in a house to eat it all, they were to invite their neighbors, provided they were circumcised, so that nothing would be left overnight. In addition, not one bone was to be broken; what remained, however, was to be burned with fire.

Exod 12

When they were about to eat, they were to stand, their clothes tucked up ready for action, white staves in their hands and shoes on their feet, like people prepared for a journey, that is, ready to leave the slavery of Egypt.

This lamb is a symbol of Christ.[7] For just as the children of Israel were saved by the blood of the lamb smeared on the lintel, and the plagues that struck the whole of Egypt did not harm them, in the same way we are saved when our hearts are smeared, washed, and purified with the blood of Christ, when we accept him and make ourselves partakers of his suffering and death. The eternal plague prepared for the whole world cannot harm us. As with the lamb, no bone of Christ's was broken when the bones of those who were crucified with him were broken. Just as the lamb was to be without blemish, so too no sin was found in Christ and no deceit in his mouth. He was killed as an innocent and spotless lamb. Now, if we want to be partakers of this lamb (the divine Word) and eat the bread of the Lord, we must eat it standing; that is, we must stand firm in faith and trust in the Lord, expecting his coming with our *Eph 6:14* clothes tucked up in readiness, girded with truth and wearing the armor of righteousness. We must have in our hands a white staff – a clear conscience toward God – as those who are purified and reconciled in him and certain of being his children, and wear on our feet the armor of the gospel of peace. *Eph 6:15* Readied like people wanting to embark on a journey, we must prepare ourselves in Christ to endure cross and death, if necessary, in passing through this vale of tears to the true fatherland.

When the people of Israel wanted to eat the lamb, they were not allowed to take leavened bread with it, but only unleavened bread. This means we must rid ourselves of all leaven – all sin and wickedness – and take a sweet bread, that is, become new creatures in Christ, well pleasing to him, as Paul teaches: "Since *1 Cor 5:7–8* we also have a paschal lamb, Christ Jesus, let us keep the feast, not with the old leaven of wickedness, but with the sweet dough of sincerity and truth." Whenever the Passover is kept and children ask their parents, "What is this; what does this mean?" their parents answer, "It is the Passover of the Lord, as in Egypt, when he slew all the firstborn in the whole land, but kept the angel of death from coming to us." Now the lamb itself is not the Passover of the Lord in Egypt, but a sign to remember it by, so that his people should not forget his loving kindness.

It was just about this lamb that the disciples *Mark 14:12–15* asked, "Where do you want us to prepare the *Luke 22:9–12* paschal lamb?" Christ said, "Go to the town and you will meet a man with two jugs of water. Follow him and say to the master of the house, 'Where can we prepare the paschal lamb?' He will show you a large, furnished room; prepare it for us there." In the evening Jesus came and sat there with the *Luke 22:15* twelve. While they were eating, he said, "I have yearned with very great longing to eat this paschal lamb with you before I suffer." (With these words he annuls the old sign and appoints a new one, namely *Matt 26:26* bread and wine.) Then after they had eaten, he took the bread and thanked his Father, and broke it. By breaking the bread in the sight of his disciples he indicated that he would break his body for them and all humanity, in order that all who believed in him might have eternal life and come to him. He said of *John 12:32* himself, "After I am lifted up from the earth, I will draw everyone to me."

"He gave it to his disciples." Through this Christ taught them that, just as after breaking the loaf he gave them bread to sustain the body, in the same way after giving up his body, he wanted to give them eternal life and redeem them from death. For through his death we receive life – as the whole of scripture says – and the true food of the Spirit, which revives, comforts, and upholds our souls.

"He said, 'Take and eat.'" Just as Christ commands his disciples to share the broken bread and eat, it is his will that we accept and share in the breaking of the true bread, that is, the suffering and death of Christ, so that we also shall share in his resurrection and glory. For Paul says, "We are God's heirs and fellow heirs with Christ if we suffer with him in order that we, too, may be raised to glory with him." *Rom 8:17*

"This is my body, which is broken for you." Paul explains clearly what the body is. He says, "We, who are many, are one loaf and one body – we who all partake of one bread." It is this body that he means, for he says in another place, "In my own person I am making up whatever is still lacking and remains to be completed of Christ's afflictions for the sake of his body, which is the church." You might say, "I understand – you attribute your blessedness to your suffering." Far be that from us! It is Christ only, as the head, who gives the whole body salvation and boldness, provided the members accept the suffering of the head in order that his friends, too, may be blessed. A branch can bear no fruit unless it shares the sap of the vine, for the sap that nourishes it all comes from the root. In the same way, all blessing comes to us from Christ, the head who sustains the whole body. *Luke 22:19* *1 Cor 10:17* *Col 1:24* *John 15:4–5*

Luke 22:19 "As often as you do this, do it in memory of me." Now as he commands us to do it in memory of him, it is clear that he himself is not there and eaten, even *Matt 26:26* though he also says, "Take, eat; this is my body." If one says, "Drink St. John's blessing," one does not mean one drinks the blessing itself, but that the wine is blessed. Similarly, the words, "Eat; this is my body" do not mean that we eat Christ's flesh and blood, but that [with the bread and wine] he demonstrates his body to us. That is why he commands us to do it in memory of him. In the same way, the lamb is not the Passover which took place in Egypt, although the Israelites told their children that it was. They did not say so because it was actually the Passover, but because the lamb reminded them to think of it and to thank God for it. Similarly, the bread is not the body, but reminds us of Christ's body – that is, it reminds us to think of his suffering and death – for he says, "As often as you do this, do it in memory of *1 Cor 11:26* me." Paul says similarly, "Proclaim the Lord's death till he comes." Thus at the Lord's Supper it is necessary to consider Christ's death and our death, and also Christ's love and our love.

THE SYMBOLS
OF BREAD AND WINE

CHRIST'S LOVE and our love are shown to us in the bread and wine.[8] Just as there are many grains of wheat, which are ground by the millstones and become flour, then baked and become bread – and in the bread we no longer distinguish one particle of flour from another – the same thing is true of us human beings, many as we are. When we are ground by the millstone of divine power, believe God's Word and submit to the cross of Christ, we are brought together, bound with the band of love to one body of which Christ is the head. As Paul puts it, "We who partake of one bread, though many, are one bread and one body." Those who truly surrender to the Lord become of one mind, heart, and soul. As the grains of corn unite in the bread, and as Christ, the head, is one with the Father, so the members are of one mind with the

1 Cor 10:17

1 Cor 2:16 head. As it is written, "We have the mind of Christ." But whoever does not have the mind of Christ is not his. And just as each grain of wheat gives the others all it has in order that there may be one loaf of bread, Christ our captain has given himself to us as *John 13:34* an example that we should love each other as he has loved us, no longer living for ourselves, but giving *1 Pet 4:10* ourselves to live for the whole body and serving the *Eph 4:16* others with the gifts we have received so that the body may grow and build itself up.

John 13:1 Now, just as Christ loved his own, he loved them unto death. Thus the Lord's Supper proclaims to us the death of Christ and our death. For as Christ broke the bread in the sight of his disciples, he later broke his body for the salvation of the whole world. In the bread Christ showed us his body broken for our salvation; we too, when we break the bread, show our willingness to give our bodies out of love, for the sake of his Word and for our brothers – strengthening and comforting them when we find them weak, whether they are in pain or in the agonies of fire or water or whatever distress, no matter what the world does *1 Cor 11:29* to us as a result. For whoever eats and drinks from the Lord's cup unworthily eats and drinks judgment upon himself. Truly, whoever eats the Lord's bread and drinks from the Lord's cup without first examining himself to see if he is ready to give his life for the truth of the gospel and for his brothers eats and drinks judgment upon himself.

What I have just said about the bread is also true of the wine, for wine is made of many grapes which are crushed in the winepress and then flow together and become wine, and one cannot recognize which grape it comes from. Since Christian unity is likewise proclaimed in the bread and in the whole practice of the Lord's Supper, however, it is not necessary to explain this symbol as well. Just see if the wafer you eat at Mass is like this or not.

CHRIST'S PRACTICE VERSUS
THAT OF THE ANTICHRIST

W HEN CHRIST had eaten the paschal lamb with his disciples, he took bread and thanked his heavenly Father. The Antichrist does not give thanks; he blesses the bread. Christ broke the bread. The Antichrist does not break it but gives a whole wafer, and if he does break it at Mass he devours all three pieces, and gives no one else anything. Christ gave it to his disciples and said, "Take." The Antichrist does not do this, but forbids people to touch it. Christ says "Eat"; the Antichrist does not. He says it is a food that must not be crushed by hands. Christ says, "This is my body, which is broken for you," but the Antichrist says it is broken every day at Mass for us and so must suffer and be sacrificed every day – opposing Paul's teaching that Christ has perfected all who should be sanctified by a single offering, and that he himself

Luke 22:19

Matt 26:26

1 Cor 11:24

Heb 10:14
Heb 1:3

has sat down at the right hand of God's throne and is sacrificed no more.

Christ says, "As often as you do this, do it in memory of me." I ask, does the word "do" mean here to bring Christ from heaven and rob him of his place beside the Father? Does "do" mean to worship the dead element, bread, or does "do" mean to banish Christ into the bread and enclose him in a little cage? On the contrary, with this word Christ tells us to think of his suffering and dying and to thank and praise the Father. When the creator of abomination wants to make a god out of bread, he says, "This is my body." Now if we should follow the letter of his words, it would have to be the priest's body and not Christ's, or he would have to change the words and say, "This is Christ's body." But if you say it stands in place of Christ, where must Christ be meanwhile? Behind the oven, perhaps? Oh, woe to the great blindness everywhere in the whole world today! They prepare only bread to house him who has built for himself a living temple to dwell in, namely the heart of those who believe.

I BELIEVE IN
THE HOLY SPIRIT

I believe in the Holy Spirit,
who builds up a Christian church,
the community of the saints,
in which there is forgiveness of sins;
I believe also in the resurrection of the body,
and eternal life.
May God help us all to it! Amen.

THE HOLY SPIRIT is the power of the Most High that brings all this about in all people. He renews the new man in the Son, brings us to know Christ and God, and reveals all the treasures of the mystery hidden in them. As Paul testifies, Christ has revealed God to us through his spirit, for the Holy Spirit searches and knows all things, even the depth of the divine being. For which man knows what is in another except the

Eph 3:4–5

1 Cor 2:10–12

spirit of man that dwells in him? Likewise, no one knows what is in God except the spirit of God. We have not received the spirit that comes from this world but the spirit that comes from God, so we are able to know what is given us by God.

Through thus revealing and imparting his gift, he brings together the church and house of God, founded and built up on Christ. She is made pure and holy by the blood of Christ, who leads all poor, miserable, battered, and worried souls with the gathering comfort of his grace into the house of God, where they receive forgiveness of sins. There they are bound together with a band of love as one *Col 3:14* body by the one Spirit who brings it all about. He is a father to the poor and miserable, strength to the weak, comfort to the mourning, a guide to the truth for those who go astray, a light to those who *Luke 1:79* sit in darkness. He raises the fallen and gives all the varied gifts of God: quiet rest to those who labor, *Matt 11:28–30* and coolness and stimulation in the heat of distress and affliction. Through him everything becomes light and easy for us to carry and endure. He leads us through and gives us victory in order to take us to the place Christ has prepared for us.

WHAT WE BELIEVE
ABOUT MARRIAGE

Gen 1

Gen 2:20–24

I N T H E B E G I N N I N G God created heaven and earth and all that lives, and finally man. As Adam found no helpmate among the creatures, God sent him into a deep sleep and then took a rib from his side and made of it a woman. When Adam awoke, God placed her before him, and seeing her, Adam said, "This is bone of my bones and flesh of my flesh, so she shall be called woman." Because of this a man will leave father and mother and cleave to his wife, and the two will become one flesh. This

Matt 19:6
tallies with what Christ says: "They are not two, but one flesh." Since they are now one flesh through their agreement to live together in love, no one can separate them, for what God has joined man must

Matt 5:32
not separate. Whoever divorces his wife, except on the grounds of adultery, commits adultery, and whoever marries a divorced woman also commits

adultery. So we know that no adulterer will have part in the kingdom of God and Christ. Thus men ought to love their wives as their own flesh. Who has ever hated his own flesh? On the contrary, one cares for it and nourishes it with great diligence.

1 Cor 6:9

Eph 5:22–33

For just as the church of God is united in marriage with Christ, so a woman is united with a man; and just as Christ cares for his church, supporting and nourishing her, men should protect, nourish, and care for their wives. Further, just as Christ loved the church, not sparing himself but giving his life for her salvation, husbands also should love their wives as their own bodies and look upon their wives' afflictions as their own. Wives should submit to their husbands as to the Lord, like Sarah, who obeyed her husband and called him lord; those women who stand firm in faith are now her daughters. Husbands, however, should treat their wives with great gentleness and kindness – as the weaker vessels, but also as their partners in the grace of God. They should live together in the love of God and do his work in pure fear of him, seeking in everything to praise him. For he who created them in the beginning said to them, "Be fruitful and multiply and fill the earth."

1 Pet 3:6–7

Gen 1:28

Thus Paul teaches that each should voluntarily perform his or her marital duty; for the husband

1 Cor 7:3–4

73

does not rule over his own body, but his wife does, and the wife does not rule over her body, but her husband does. But I say, where there is no marital *Tb 6:17* duty, we should refrain in order that we do not live like horses and mules without understanding, but as those who have been made holy by the blood of Christ and have died to all fleshly lust. Paul also *1 Cor 7:29* says, "Let those who have wives live as those who *Matt 19:12* have none." And Jesus says, "He who is able to accept this, let him." So I say if a man wants to marry, he should go about it carefully, and see that he does not do so in order to please the lust of the flesh; for *Heb 13:4* it is written, "Let the marriage bed be undefiled." Let it take place out of God's love and love to children, as Tobit shows us.[9] As the angel said to the *Tb 6:16–17* young Tobias, "I will tell you over whom the devil has power: over those who marry more out of fleshly lust than out of God's love and love to children." So let those who marry do so in the fear of God. In this way each will learn the will of God. What a blessing marriage is if it is kept in a godly way as befits the saints; but what a wretched thing when not kept as God and Christ intended! It is no better than fornication in God's sight.

Let the wife be subject to her husband in all that *1 Cor 11:3* is right, and the husband be the head of his wife; and

let the wife revere her husband, but not the husband   *Eph 5:33*
his wife, for the man was not made for the woman,   *1 Cor 11:9*
but the woman for the man's sake. Adam was not   *1 Tim 2:14*
the first to transgress, but Eve, who brought on the
curse. Yet neither can man exist without woman   *1 Cor 11:11–12*
nor woman without man, for just as woman came
from man, man also comes through woman, and
everything from God. So the wife should obey her   *Eph 5:22–29*
husband, but the husband should love his wife.
Whoever hates his wife hates himself. For a good   *Prov 12:4*
wife is the crown of her husband, strength for his
bones, and an adornment to his house.

HOW WE SHOULD BUILD UP
THE HOUSE OF GOD AND
WHAT THE HOUSE OF GOD IS

Luke 14:28–29

CHRIST SAYS that anyone who wants to build a tower or a house first sits down and considers the cost – to see whether or not he has enough to finish building. If he finds he does not have enough, he does not build, for he does not want to lay the foundation and then have to stop, and be laughed to scorn, with everyone saying, "He began to build a house but cannot finish it." It is the same with us: if we begin building for eternal life, we must first count the cost. Will we find ourselves able to bear all that meets us and is laid upon us for the sake of God and Christ? Can we endure and suffer persecution and contempt to gain him? Can we strangle the flesh with all its lusts, leave the world with all its pleasures and splendor, and with-

stand the devil and all his wickedness to guard the
precious treasure, Christ? Now, if we find we are
able, we can begin to build joyfully on the foundation of all the apostles, whose cornerstone is Christ.
Paul says, "No one can lay any foundation other   *1 Cor 3:10–15*
than the one that is already laid, which is Christ."[10]
Like a wise master builder I have laid a foundation
through God's grace, and now another may build
upon it. But each should take care how he build
on it, for he will receive his wages according to his
work – whether good or bad. That is why Peter says,
"You have come to the living stone, rejected by the   *1 Pet 2:4–5*
builders – that is, by the scribes – but in God's sight
chosen and precious. Let yourselves also be built as
living stones into a living temple of God, that he
may live and do his work in you."

But if one wants to build a fine house, one must
hew the stone, and we likewise must circumcise and   *Deut 10:16*
purify our hearts from all sin and unrighteousness
as Peter teaches: "Put away all malice and cunning,   *1 Pet 2:1–2*
slander and hypocrisy, and desire pure spiritual milk
(that is, the living Word of God) like a newborn
babe, so that in it you may grow." In this way you
can adorn the house with precious stones, so that it
is inviting, clean, and pleasing for the Father to live

in. But such hewing of the stone can take place only through much tribulation and persecution for the Word's sake, as it is written: "Whoever has suffered in the flesh has ceased from sin."

But today everyone says, "Oh, there is still time. I must first get my house in order, see to my business and my family, and support my friends." Of such people the Lord says through the prophets, "This nation says the time has not yet come to rebuild the house of the Lord." But he answers them: "Is this the time for you to sit in your paneled houses, while my house lies in ruins?" Yes, it is truly so over the whole world that people live willfully and seek only how to fill their coffers in order to beautify their houses and properties more extravagantly for their enjoyment and pleasure. They do not think of the poor or how they might show them love. They would sooner leave them to be eaten by maggots under a fence than go to help them. Therefore the Lord says, "They eat much but are not satisfied"; that is, although they often hear the truth, they are not satisfied with it and don't put it into deed and live accordingly as children of God. They are forever studying, but cannot reach true knowledge because their hearts are darkened. They drink much, yet never become drunk with the sweet wine of the knowledge and

1 Pet 4:1

Hag 1:2–3

Hos 4:10

2 Tim 3:7

wisdom of God, that is, with the Holy Spirit, whom they are unable to receive on account of their disbelief and malice. They clothe themselves, yet have no warmth; that is, they boast about truth and faith, but their faith is weak and dead in God's sight since it does not give itself to be fruitful in love. When they receive wages, they keep them in a purse with holes – that is, though they receive from God the gift of the knowledge of Christ, they do not perceive it but think little of it. Just as those who keep their money in a purse with holes lose it and find nothing when they are in need, likewise those who receive a gift from God and do not perceive it and increase it – who think little of it and hide it because they are afraid of the world – will find that the Lord will take it away. He will give it instead to those who are faithful and spare no effort, but work hard to build the house of the Lord with the gift given them.

That is why the Lord, who desires his house to be built, commands, "Climb the mountain and get wood for my house, so I may dwell there and be gracious to you and serve you honorably – otherwise, though you expect much, you shall receive little; even if you take it home I shall blow it away, because my house lies waste." This mountain is Christ, as scripture testifies: "I saw a stone cut out from the

Hag 1:6

Luke 19:20–26
Matt 25:24–29

Hag 1:8–9

Dan 2:34–35

mountain by no human hand, and the stone became a great mountain and filled the whole earth and was set upon Mount Zion, raised above all mountains and hills." We must climb this mountain through faith and firm trust in Christ, and take with us the wood, that is, receive from him the gift of the Holy Spirit, which he has promised all who love him. He

John 16:7, 13–14

said, "When I go I shall send you the Comforter, the Holy Spirit, who will teach you the whole truth; for he will take what is mine and proclaim it to you." When Christ says that the Spirit will take the truth from what is his and proclaim it to us, he testifies that in him there is the whole fullness of divine

John 1:16

nature, from which, as John says, we all receive grace upon grace. Through such wood, namely the grace of the Holy Spirit, the house of the Lord is built, in which he wants to live and be gracious to us. This

1 Cor 3:16–17

house is the church of God. Paul tells us, "You are the temple of the living God, and whoever desecrates it he will shame, for his temple is holy, and you

2 Cor 6:16–18

are that temple." As God says, "I will live in them and move among them and be their God, and they shall be my people." Therefore he says, "Come out from among the unbelievers and be separate from them, and touch nothing unclean; then I will accept you and be your father, and you shall be my sons and daughters."

David also tells us about this house, "One thing I have asked of the Lord, and will I seek: that I may dwell in his house all the days of my life." And again he says, "I will speak of your name to my brethren and sing praise to you in the congregation." This house, the church, is not built by men but by God, and Christ has become its guardian and head. God, who is the builder of this house and who knows all things, knew beforehand the rushing violence of the strong winds and the great floods that will beat against it, and so that it may withstand them, he has fortified it upon the firm foundation of Christ, against which all the powers of hell can do nothing. He has also surrounded it with unshakable pillars, so that it may be protected and not fall when the winds and floods of tribulation beat against it.

Ps 27:4

Ps 22:22

Eph 1:22

Matt 16:18

T HE FIRST PILLAR of this house is the
pure fear of God, for as it is written, "The
fear of God is the beginning of wisdom."
Against this pillar beat the mighty wind and dam-
aging water of the fear of men, showing us how
Christians are treated. The king and his lords will
not tolerate you; they will drive you from house and
home, wife and children, take everything that is
yours, and rob you of your life as well. People say,
"Oh, you will never hold out against such things;
leave well enough alone and be content." We must
withstand this, however, in the fear of God, and
must fear God more than men, as Christ teaches
us, saying, "Have no fear of those who kill the body
but cannot do anything more; rather fear him who,
after he has killed, has power to cast body and soul
to destruction." Moreover, Esdras says, "They will

Ps 111:10

Prov 1:7; 9:10

Matt 10:28

2 Esd 16:72–73

drive you from house and home and rob you of your goods. That shall be the time of testing for the faithful." Do not let this make you afraid; for there is no one, Christ says, "who has left house, home, meadow, field, wife, child, father, mother, sister, or brother for my name's sake and for the gospel's, who will not receive it again many times over in this world, and in the world to come, life everlasting." *Mark 10:29–30*

The second pillar of this house is the wisdom of God, for he who fears God will know wisdom. Against this pillar beat the mighty wind and destructive water of the wisdom of people who say, "It is a foolish thing to voluntarily go into danger." To them the teaching of the cross is foolishness. They say, "How can it be right when no one follows it except simple folk who are led astray?" But even though a wise man or a scribe or a rich person thinks in this way, we must oppose him with the wisdom of God, which is Christ, who was despised by all. Wisdom must be vindicated by all its children. Paul says, "The wisdom of God is foolishness to the world, for it cannot be recognized by worldly wisdom." The foolishness of God, however, is wiser than the world with all its knowledge, so we must use it to strive against the world; its wisdom is foolishness in God's eyes. For this reason not many *1 Cor 1:18–25*

Luke 7:35

of the wise of this world are called, as is written: "Where are the wise men? Where are the scribes? Where are the debaters? Has not God put to shame the wisdom of this world?" And again, "The Lord knows the thoughts of the wise, that they are foolishness." And also, "The Lord traps the wise in their own cleverness." Therefore Christ says, "I thank you, Father, Lord of heaven and earth, that you have hidden these things from the wise and the scribes and revealed them to little children; yes, Father, for such was your gracious will."

Ps 94:11

Job 5:13
Matt 11:25–26

The third pillar of this house is God's understanding. Against this pillar beats the mighty wind of human understanding, which wants to consider and recognize everything in its arrogance and says, "This is an intelligent man. You will not easily find his equal – he is so well versed in scripture and is such a good commentator that he must also understand it correctly." But we must oppose him with God's understanding and not listen to him who follows his own wishes and does not follow Christ. For God says, "I will destroy the wisdom of the wise, and the cleverness of the clever I will thwart." Because all human understanding is empty and useless, we should consider only that which comes down from above, from the Father of lights, with whom there

1 Cor 1:19
Isa 29:14

Jas 1:17

is no variation or change due to darkness. Christ says, "You must be taught by God. Everyone who has heard and learned from my Father comes to me." *John 6:45* As Paul says, we must never make people a cause for pride, but await all knowledge from God; that is, the understanding that comes from God himself. For if the Spirit of God himself gives understanding, and scripture is explained by scripture, nothing will be mistaken or misunderstood. *1 Cor 3:21* *Job 32:8*

The fourth pillar of this house is the counsel of God. Against this pillar beats the mighty wind of human counsel, of people who come and say: "You are a fine person; you can yet come to something – become a well-regarded man or woman, raise children, and at the same time serve God. Don't you see, you are guilty of harming yourself [by your belief]; it is just as if you were strangling yourself. Don't do it! Can't you see that we want to be saved too? And if this doesn't happen right away, after all, God is merciful. Besides, Christ has done enough for our sins. What need do we have of all that? If one only believes, everything is already put right. Keep your ideas to yourself – why should you tell everyone what you believe?"

We must withstand all this human counsel with the counsel of Christ, who asks, "What will it profit *Matt 16:26* a person if he gains the whole world and suffers harm to his own soul, or what will he give to redeem his soul?" He also says, "You will be despised by all people," and "He who seeks his own life will lose it, but he who loses his life for my sake will find it." Further, "No one comes to the Father but by me." "You share in Christ, provided you hold firmly to your beginning in his nature." And, "I am God, who visits the iniquities of the fathers upon the children to the third and fourth generation of those who hate me, and shows mercy to thousands who love my name." And, "We have become heirs with Christ, provided we suffer with him in order that we may also be glorified with him." And, "People believe with their hearts, and so become upright; they confess with their lips and so are saved."

Matt 10:22

Matt 10:39

John 14:6

Heb 3:14

Exod 20:5–6

Rom 8:17

Rom 10:10

The fifth pillar of this house is the might of God. Against this pillar beats the powerful wind of human might and power, which speaks thus: "Look, how are you going to carry this out? The whole world is against you. Do you really think you can fight against the whole world? See how kings, lords, and all the powerful persecute you in order to kill you." We must withstand such words with the might and power of God, for Christ says, "My Father is stronger than all the world, and no one

John 10:29

is able to snatch anyone out of his hand." He also
says, "Be of good cheer; I have overcome the world."   *John 16:33*
And again, "He who is in you is greater than he who   *1 John 4:4*
is in the world." As it is written, "Even the hairs of   *Matt 10:30*
your head are numbered, and not one will fall from
you without your Father knowing it, so do not be
afraid." David says, "It is better to put confidence in   *Ps 118: 8–9*
God than in princes; it is better to trust God than
to rely on man." So do not put your trust in princes
or in the children of men, for they cannot help you.
Again, "God smites all our enemies upon the cheek   *Ps 3:7*
and breaks the teeth of the wicked." If God be for   *Rom 8:31*
us, who can be against us? No one, for with the Lord   *Ps 27:1*
there is salvation.

The sixth pillar of this house is the knowledge
of God. Against this pillar beats the mighty wind
of human knowledge, which claims to know much
and to be capable of many things; yet, as Paul says,
"Those who imagine they know much do not yet   *1 Cor 8:1–2*
know as they ought to know. Knowledge puffs up,
but love edifies." They come and say, "Do you really
think cobblers and tailors know more than those
who have studied the arts all their lives and are
learned and well practiced in them?"[12] Paul answers
this when he says, "Claiming to be wise, they became   *Rom 1:22*
fools." For the word and knowledge of God is not

learned in schools of higher education, but as Christ

John 6:45 says, "Whoever hears and learns from my Father comes to me." We must, therefore, reject all human knowing so that we may attain true knowledge. Such may be learned only in the school of the Father's discipline, which we must enter as David did. As God

Isa 28:9 says through the prophets, "To whom will I teach my wisdom but to those weaned from milk?" With this knowledge we must strive against everything that is in the world, so that we may await the Bridegroom, Christ, and be ready when he comes. We must put aside all this world's wisdom in order to gain the true

1 Cor 3:18 knowledge of God. As Paul says, "If anyone among you desires to be wise, let him first become a fool, that he may become truly wise."

The seventh pillar of this house is the favor or friendship of God. If a person overcomes all these things, he will be called a friend of God. Against this pillar beat the mighty wind and destructive water of the friendship and favor of the world, love of possessions, arrogant living, and the like. A person who strives for these and other trappings of wealth

John 15:19 is loved by the world – as Christ says, "The world loves her own" – but we must withstand such friendship with the grace and love of God and beware of

Jas 4:4 it. For it is written, "Whoever wants to be a friend of

God must be an enemy of the world, for friendship with the world is enmity to God." Again, friendship with God is enmity to the world. And so Christ says, *John 15:19* "If you were of the world, the world would love you, but because you are not of the world, the world hates you." He says, "It will come to pass that whoever *John 16:2* kills you will think he is offering service to God." We must be hated by all people for his name's sake *Matt 10:22* in order to overcome all things through the grace and love of God; for if we love him with our hearts, everything that is laid upon us for his name's sake will become easy for us to bear. Therefore he says, "Blessed are you when you are persecuted, for your *Luke 6:22–23* release will come." Those who endure in all this will find that their work will stand and not be consumed, *1 Cor 3:12–15* even if tested by fire. Christ will come and hold his *Rev 3:20–21* Supper with them and grant them to sit with him on his throne, as he himself has conquered and sat with his Father on his throne. May the power of God help us thus to overcome! Amen.

You children of Lot, go out from Sodom, that you may not receive her plagues.

Written in the prison at Gmunden in the land on the Enns.[13]

———

RIEDEMANN'S ODE TO LOVE

Werner O. Packull

BY ALL ACCOUNTS Peter Riedemann was a most remarkable Hutterite who survived nine years in sixteenth-century prisons, in itself a remarkable feat. But he did more than survive. While imprisoned at Gmunden, Nuremberg, Marburg, and Wolkersdorf, he wrote the most substantive defense of faith on behalf of his community. Indeed, his prison experiences at Nuremberg and Marburg proved invaluable, because they required an encounter with trained theologians against whom he defended the views of his community.

Leading scholars agree that this gifted young shoemaker provided the Anabaptist Hutterites

This essay is taken from Werner Packull's Peter Riedemann: Shaper of the Hutterite Tradition.[14]

with an apology that has remained normative for the community into the present. Johann Loserth considered Riedemann's *Confession of Faith* "the most coherent doctrinal statement" of the Hutterite community,[15] while Robert Friedmann described Riedemann's work as "the finest document on Anabaptist faith and conduct." He ranked Riedemann second in importance to the Hutterite movement only to the founding father of the Hutterites, Jacob Hutter.[16] Leonard Gross went further, venturing to say that Riedemann's *Confession of Faith* constituted "the most perfectly balanced expression" of Hutterite faith and practice, indeed of sixteenth-century Anabaptism as a whole.[17] And George Williams echoed the consensus of scholars when he designated Riedemann the "outstanding doctrinal writer" and "second founder" of the Hutterite brotherhood.[18]. . .

Riedemann's biography reaches beyond the turbulent beginnings to second-generation consolidation and institutionalization. His influence was both foundational and tradition-shaping, tasks continued by Peter Walpot after Riedemann's death. Riedemann's emphasis on strong leadership assured a smooth transition to the next generation and beyond at critical points of Hutterite survival and identity formation. His masterly *Confession of Faith,* coupled with his stress on leadership, became normative for the Hutterite tradition, while his earlier *Gmunden Confession,*[19] his epistles, and his songs remain inspirational for the community.[20] These sources also permit insight into the evolution of young Riedemann from journeyman shoemaker to Hutterite spiritual leader.

UNFORTUNATELY, little is known about the circumstances leading to Riedemann's arrest and imprisonment in Gmunden, Upper Austria, but the martyrdom of two women in Gmunden during 1528 suggests that Anabaptism had spread to the city earlier that year. . . .

During the investigation following his arrest in November 1529, Riedemann was subjected to severe torture that left him near death. He survived, no doubt partly due to his youthful resilience, even though he remained in Gmunden's prison for three years and four weeks.[21] Then, through the "providence of God" and perhaps the assistance of the shoemaker Thoman, he regained his freedom.[22] The Hutterite *Chronicle* records simply that:

. . . toward the end of 1532 a Servant of the Word, Peter Riedemann, a native of Hirschberg in Silesia, came from Upper Austria. For more than three years he had been in prison there at Gmunden, subjected to great pain, hunger, and mistreatment. But he persevered in his faith and was released.[23]

No explanation is provided for Reidemann's release. He arrived at the community in Auspitz, Moravia, on New Year's Eve in 1533, bringing with him literature he had apparently penned in prison. Robert Friedmann, who examined its content, labelled these writings somewhat euphemistically a "confession of faith." If these were in fact written in prison, then the conditions of Riedemann's imprisonment during the latter stages at Gmunden must have been quite different from the near-death experience he underwent at the beginning. Indeed, he must have been well enough to write, and in possession of paper, pen, and ink. But whatever the circumstances of his stay at Gmunden, the manuscript he brought out of prison provides an opportunity to gauge his early ideas, concerns, and commitments.[24] . . .

To call Riedemann's Gmunden writings a "confession" is somewhat of a misnomer. Friedmann, who edited Riedemann's work, noted that "a disproportionately large space was given to biblical history." He suggested further that the "living experience of an ordered community life" seemed missing, although the theme of love gave these early writings a structure of sorts. The English translators took up this theme and entitled the collective work *Love Is Like Fire* – an ingenious title, because this work has the earmarks of youthful ardor for restoring pristine Christian practices. But the imposition of love as the unifying theme can also mislead us when seeking a strictly historical assessment of the work's contents, for upon closer inspection the *Gmunden Confession* is a composite of topical homilies, devotional meditations, and biblical expositions that grew out of existential concerns. The document's composite nature further suggests that its various parts originated over time with distinct interests or issues in mind. If the whole originated in prison, as generally assumed, then it must have been written during the latter part of Riedemann's tenure there.[25]

Anyone who approaches the Gmunden work expecting to find a finely honed confession or systemic theological statements will be disappointed. But it must be remembered that it is the effort of a journeyman shoemaker, not of a scholastically or humanistically educated theologian. If anything, this makes Riedemann's early work all the more interesting, for it brings the reader closer to his original concerns and the spirituality of this young layman and the movement he embodied.

Compared with Riedemann's magnum opus, the *Confession of Faith* (written some ten years later in Hesse), the *Gmunden Confession* lacks organizational focus and reveals certain spiritualist tendencies. Riedemann is fond of allegory, which contrasts with the narrative sections and literalist tendencies of the *Confession of Faith.* Later in life, however, he seemed to return to this fondness for allegory, hinted at in the eulogy of the Hutterite *Chronicle.* The *Chronicle* records that he was "a man inspired and highly gifted . . . rich in all the secrets of God" and that "the gift of God's Word flowed from him like running water, brimming over" so that he "filled all who heard him with joy."[26] As noted below, the *Chronicle's* eulogy did not exaggerate. As Martin Rothkegel discovered, Riedemann had mastered among other things the art of allegorically paraphrasing the Gospels.[27]

Turning to the structure of the *Gmunden Confession,* we should note that its English translators superimposed twenty-two subheadings on the corpus, thus creating more structural coherence than warranted in the original text. Closer examination reveals that the original work divides into five distinct composites. The first part comments upon the Apostolic Creed and begins with the Genesis account of creation. It includes and combines homilies on love and faith, and a discussion on baptism and the errors of infant baptism. This section closes with the benediction: "May the eternal God, our compassionate Father . . . open the eyes and ears of your mind, that you may see and know his eternal will written in your hearts. Amen" (pages 36–37).

The second part resumes the commentary on the Apostolic Creed (pages 38–71), dealing with articles on God, Christ, the Holy Spirit, and the church. The editors have subdivided and organized the article on God with subheadings on "the fall of man" and "a parable." The article on Christ is provided with five subheadings, all concerned with the Eucharist: what eating Christ's flesh means; the error of the Mass; what we believe about the Lord's Supper; the symbol of bread and wine; Christ versus Antichrist.

Surprisingly, the joint articles on the Spirit and the church receive rather short treatment.

Next follows a homily on "What we believe about marriage." Two separate but related tracts, "How one should build the house of God" and "The seven pillars of this house," allegorically address the restoration of the church (pages 76–89). The explication of the seven pillars seems reminiscent of a pamphlet attributed to Jörg Haugk von Jüchsen, an ally of the early Anabaptist, Hans Hut. But unlike Haugk, who focused on a seven-fold inner purgation, Riedemann's seven pillars represent metaphors for rebuilding the true church.[28]

It is highly unlikely that Riedemann wrote these various composite parts in their present arrangement or sequence. Some parts, such as the tract on marriage, address specific issues that do not seem to belong in the present ordering but were freestanding. Riedemann's concern with marriage was possibly prompted by issues that had divided the community. A schism had taken place while Riedemann was still in Gmunden's prison. Accusations of unfair marriage arrangements and the alleged neglect of the community's children were among the reasons cited for the rift.[29] Riedemann's lengthy admonition to brotherly love, in turn, can be read as his response to reports of factionalism in the recently founded Anabaptist communities of Moravia, news of which must have reached him while he was still in prison.

The exposition of the Apostolic Creed, on the other hand, may have been prompted by external factors. More than two years before Riedemann's arrest in Gmunden, Ferdinand I had decreed adherence to the creed and to the seven sacraments a minimal standard of orthodoxy for his territories.[30] Riedemann's commentary on the creed, at the core of his Gmunden work, may thus have originated in response to his examination by local clergy or officials at Gmunden.[31] Generally, the creed was held in high esteem by Anabaptists as a summary of scriptural teachings and as genuinely apostolic. Not surprisingly, Riedemann returns to it repeatedly.

BY CALLING THIS BOOK *Love Is Like Fire,* the editors suggest love as the dominant theme for the entire document. There is much to be said for this view, because Riedemann compared divine love to sunlight and fire; to an overflowing spring; to the care of a loving, nurturing mother; and to birds caring for their young. Daily bread, drink, shelter, and strength of body he considered to be gifts of a loving God. He believed that God's love revealed in Christ inspired love for the divine commandments and Christian ordinances as well as love of neighbor. Admittedly, the love of God had not yet come to full fruition in the congregation of God. It seemed necessary therefore to admonish members not to grumble or complain, to avoid proud, conceited language, and to converse graciously with each other. He reminded his readers that love of neighbor did not seek its own advantage (page 17), but apparently he did not as yet advocate community of goods. His language of becoming one with brothers and sisters in Christ seems to put priority on like-mindedness in the fellowship. As previously noted, some of his earlier statements remain difficult to contextualize and lack congregational concreteness. His call for neighborly love seems to extend beyond a single community. Answering the rhetorical question, "Who is my neighbor?" he pointed to the example of the good Samaritan (page 18) and suggested that "we are all one another's neighbor – the one who needs help and the one who offers help. No one is excluded." All need love and all need to pass it on. "Love flows from faith; for where there is no faith there cannot be love, and where there is no love there cannot be faith. The two are so entwined that one cannot be pleasing to God without the other" (page 22).

Thus Riedemann linked faith and love as the saving virtues in the divine–human drama. Without faith and love, relationships with one another and with the neighbor could not prosper. Coming from a young shoemaker who experienced torture and imprisonment, this ode to love seems all the more surprising and poignant.

NOTES

1. Peter Rideman, *Rechenschaft unserer Religion, Lehr und Glaubens, von den Brüdern, so man die Hutterischen nennt, ausgegangen 1565* (Ashton Keynes, England: Cotswold Bruderhof, 1938); Available in English as *Peter Riedemann's Hutterite Confession of Faith*, trans. and ed. by John J. Friesen (Scottdale, PA: Herald Press, 1999) (hereafter *Confession of Faith*.)

2. *The Chronicle of the Hutterian Brethren*, vol. 1 (Rifton, NY: Plough, 1987), 84.

3. See *Mennonite Quarterly Review*, July 1991. For a fuller discussion of Riedemann's life and work, see Werner O. Packull, *Peter Riedemann: Shaper of the Hutterite Tradition* (Kitchener, ON: Pandora Press, 2007).

4. *Chronicle*, 330.

5. See Hans Hut, "Ein christlich Unterrichtung" (1526–27), in Lydia Müller, ed., *Glaubenszeugnisse oberdeutscher Taufgesinnter,* vol. 1 (Leipzig, 1938), 33, 67.

6. Here, following Friedmann's German edition, a lengthy section of Riedemann's text, mainly a retelling of stories from the Old Testament, has been omitted.

7. Still today the Hutterites use a sixteenth-century sermon on Exodus 12 in their preparation for celebrating the Lord's Supper.

8. The following parable was popular among the Anabaptists, especially the Hutterites. Cf. *Chronicle,* 258; Peter Walpot, "True Surrender and Community of Goods," in *Mennonite Quarterly Review* (Jan. 1957), 45–46; Andreas Ehrenpreis, *Sendbrief* (Scottdale, PA, 1920); Lydia Müller, *Der Kommunismus der Mährischen Wiedertäufer* (Leipzig, 1938), 66. The parable appears for the first time in the *Didache,* or "Teaching of the Twelve Apostles," ca. AD 120 (see Eberhard Arnold, ed., *The Early Christians in Their Own Words* (Walden, NY: Plough, 1997), 200–201); it also appears in Martin Luther's book *Von der deutschen Messe* (1519).

9. The Book of Tobit in the Apocrypha, especially Tobit 8:9, is often quoted by Anabaptists in connection with marriage; it is still popular among the Amish today.

10. This was later Menno Simons's motto.

11. The biblical source of this allegory is Proverbs 9:1: "Wisdom has built her house, and she has set up her seven pillars." It seems that

Riedemann took the main idea from a tract which the peasant leader Jörg Haugk von Juchsen published in 1524 with the title, "A Christian Order, or the Beginning of a Christian Life"; see excerpts in Lydia Müller, *Glaubenszeugnisse* I, 3–10. In this writing Jörg Haugk teaches that "a Christian life follows rungs or steps until it reaches perfection," and that there are seven such rungs. The "seven grades to perfection" are the spirit of the fear of God, the spirit of wisdom, the spirit of understanding, the spirit of counsel, the spirit of strength, the spirit of knowledge, and the spirit of godliness. In Riedemann's tract we find the first six pillars with the same names, but for the seventh pillar he has "God's favor and friendship" where Jörg Haugk has "godliness." The basis of this enumeration is clearly Isaiah 11:2, where six of these qualities are named: the spirit of wisdom, of understanding, of counsel, of strength, of knowledge, and of the fear of the Lord.

12. The "arts" (*freien kuensten*) Riedemann refers to are the *septem artes liberales* or seven liberal arts, which we today call in general terms "the sciences."

13. Some manuscripts have the additional words "Im 1530er jar. Peter Rideman." The Brünn codex has neither date nor signature.

14. Werner O. Packull, *Peter Riedemann: Shaper of the Hutterite Tradition* (Kitchener, ON: Pandora Press, 2007), 9–10, 16–20, 32.

15. Johann Loserth, "Der Kommunismus der mährischen Wiedertäufer im 16. und 17. Jahrhundert: Beiträge zu ihrer Geschichte, Lehre und Verfassung," *Archiv für österreichische Geschichte,* 81 (1894): 137–322, esp. 167–68.

16. Robert Friedmann, ed., "Riedemann (Rideman), Peter (der 'grosse Peter' genannt)" in *Die Schriften der Hutterischen Täufergemeinschaften. Gesamtkatalog ihrer Manuscriptbücher, ihrer Schreiber und ihrer Literatur, 1526–1667* (Vienna: Verlag Hermann Böhlaus, 1965), 123; also "Peter Riedemann: An Early Anabaptist Leader," *Mennonite Quarterly Review* 44 (1970): 5–44 and "Riedemann, Peter," *Mennonite Encyclopedia* vol. 4 (Hillsboro, KS: Mennonite Brethren Pub. House, 1959), 326–28.

17. Leonard Gross, *The Golden Years of the Hutterites* (Scottdale, PA: Herald Press, 1980), 196.

18. George Williams, *The Radical Reformation* (Kirksville, MO: Sixteenth Century Journal Publishers, 1992), 646.

19. "Ein Rechenschafft und Bekandtnuss des Glaubens vom Peter Ridemann" (hereafter *Gmunden Confession*).

20. His epistles have been published in *Die Hutterischen Episteln,* vols. 1–4 (Elie, MB: James Valley Book Center, 1986, 1987, 1988, 1991). At least thirty-eight epistles have survived. In addition, forty-six songs have been attributed to Riedemann. See Ursula Lieseberg, *Die Lieder des Peter Riedemann. Studien zum Liedgut der Täufer im 16. Jahrhundert* (Frankfurt: Peter Lang, 1998), *Europäische Hochschulschriften, Reihe 1, Deutsche Sprache und Literatur,* vol. 1692.

21. Josef Beck, *Geschichtsbücher der Wiedertäufer* (Nieuwkoop, Netherlands: de Graaf, 1967), 206. Early modern prisons were notoriously porous, especially if someone on the outside cared for the prisoner.

22. He was in the beggar's or shoemaker's tower, next to a shoemaker shop; also Beck, *Geschichtsbücher der Wiedertäufer,* 40, 89.

23. *Chronicle,* 31.

24. For an index of Reidemann's epistles and songs, see Bruno Fast and Werner O. Packull, "An Index of Peter Riedemann's Epistles," *Mennonite Quarterly Review* 65 (1991): 340–51.

25. *Chronicle,* 94.

26. *Chronicle,* 330.

27. Martin Rothkegel, "Learned in the School of David: Peter Riedemann's Paraphrases of the Gospels" in *Commoners and Community: Essays in Honour of Werner O. Packull,* ed. C. Arnold Snyder (Kitchener, ON: Pandora Press, 2002), 233–56.

28. Friedmann believed the "main idea" came from Haugk, whose work was copied into Hutterite codices. [See note 11 above.] I prefer to think of parallels between Haugk's work and Riedemann. Robert Friedmann, ed., *Glaubenszeugnisse oberdeutscher Taufgesinnter,* vol. 2 (Gütersloh: Verlag Gerd Mohn, 1967), x.

29. Cf. Packull, *Hutterite Beginnings* (Baltimore: Johns Hopkins University Press, 1995), 214–235.

30. Cf. *Ibid.,* 189.

31. An inference from Riedemann's response to interrogators in Marburg. Studies are needed on the organization of materials in codices. Treatises were not bound in chronological sequence. Additions were often placed at the beginning rather than at the end of codices.

PLOUGH SPIRITUAL GUIDES
backpack classics for modern pilgrims

The Prayer God Answers
EBERHARD ARNOLD *and* RICHARD FOSTER
Rediscover the kind of prayer that has the power to transform our lives and our world.

The Two Ways
The Early Christian Vision of Discipleship
from the *Shepherd of Hermas* and the *Didache*
Find out what following Jesus meant for first-century Christians with these earliest writings of the post-apostolic era.

Now Is Eternity
Comfort and Wisdom for Difficult Hours
J. C. BLUMHARDT *and* C. F. BLUMHARDT
This collection of short meditations on God's faithfulness will help you battle weariness and despair.

Why We Live in Community
EBERHARD ARNOLD *and* THOMAS MERTON
In this time-honored manifesto Arnold and Merton join the vital discussion of what community is all about: a great adventure of faith shared with others.

Plough Publishing House
1-800-521-8011 ◆ 845-572-3455
PO BOX 398 ◆ Walden, NY 12586 ◆ USA
Brightling Rd ◆ Robertsbridge ◆ East Sussex TN32 5DR ◆ UK
4188 Gwydir Highway ◆ Elsmore, NSW 2360 ◆ Australia

www.plough.com